Descartes

Descartes

Harry M. Bracken

ONEWORLD PHILOSOPHERS

ONEWORLD

OXFORD

DESCARTES

Oneworld Publications
(Sales and Editorial)
185 Banbury Road
Oxford OX2 7AR
England
www.oneworld-publications.com

© Harry M. Bracken 2002

ISBN 1–85168–294–5

Cover design by the Bridgewater Book Company
Cover image © Bettman/CORBIS
Typeset by Saxon Graphics Ltd, Derby, UK
Printed and bound by Clays Ltd, St Ives plc

Contents

Preface

Gregor Sebba's monumental *Bibliographia Cartesiana: A Critical Guide to the Descartes Literature 1800–1960*, appeared in 1964. It contains 510 pages and 3612 entries. It is not merely a check–list of books and articles on or about Descartes, but a significant portion of it is an annotated bibliography – rich in critical comment and material. Numerous less exhaustive bibliographies have appeared in the interim. I mention this not to frighten readers but merely to underscore the breadth and the quantity of Cartesian studies over the past two centuries. I have not surveyed the wide range of Cartesian material nor even the major points of contention among philosophers. I have instead tried to provide an introduction to several of Descartes's central philosophical ideas by first giving a quick and brief picture of the world in which he wrote. Then, while spelling out some of his ideas, I have given a wide range of quotations from his texts. Finally, I have tried to provide some understanding of the hostility which Descartes continues, even after three and a half centuries, to generate. I try to give a partial answer to the question, why is Descartes *the philosopher philosophers love to hate?*

I wish to add a word of thanks to those who have helped me in various ways at various times: Charles Benson, George Elder Davie, Patrick Hyde Kelly, Elly van Gelderen, Jan Koster, Laura Parsons, Richard H. Popkin,

Walter Rex, William R. Shea, Mel Thompson, and Richard Watson.

Because of ready accessibility I have generally used the translations found in *The Philosophical Works of Descartes*, translated by Elizabeth S. Haldane and G.R.T. Ross (hereafter HR), Cambridge: University Press, 1911 f. To facilitate cross-referencing for readers who may use another translation, I try to give the locations of all citations in the Adam and Tannery edition, *Oeuvres de Descartes* (AT). For the few passages not translated in HR, I generally use the translations in John Cottingham, Robert Stoothoff, Dugald Murdoch, and Anthony Kenny (CSMK), *The Philosophical Writings of Descartes*, 3 vols, Cambridge: University Press, 1984–91.

Apache Junction, Arizona
Harry McFarland Bracken

"In the beginning..."

Although René Descartes is often called the "father of modern philosophy," he has been attacked, reviled, and condemned like no other thinker for most of the last 350 years. Even Pope John Paul II has recently felt the need to criticize him. Refutations continue to pile up. European philosophy is haunted by Descartes and his ideas. One of his most important ideas is his *rationalism*, that is, that the human mind makes a major contribution to knowledge by means of innate ideas. The mind is understood to be structured by a range of principles which are not derived from sense experience. Sense experience may be required to "trigger" aspects of our mental structures, but sense experience alone cannot yield knowledge. That, in turn, generates an account of human nature. Rationalism is usually taken to stand in opposition to *empiricism*, the view that all our knowledge is derived from sense experience. Empiricism generates a very different theory of human nature. These two different doctrines about human nature generate considerable controversy, much of it both fierce and bitter. In the pages that follow I shall briefly provide some historical background. Then the core of Descartes's philosophy will be formulated. Finally, some of the factors behind the controversy, and the primary reasons why Descartes became the primary target of criticism over the last three and a half centuries will be explored.

First, a few biographical words on Descartes's background. He was born into a family of the minor aristocracy on 31 March 1596 at La Haye (now Descartes!) in Touraine, France. His mother died in May 1597 and he was raised in the home of his maternal grand-mother (who died in 1610). He does not seem to have had a close relationship with his father.

> His father had little sympathy with Descartes or with what he achieved, and is reported as having said, on the publication of Descartes' first book, the *Discours* and accompanying essays, in 1637 "Only one of my children has displeased me. How can I have engendered a son stupid enough to have had himself bound in calf?"[1]

He studied at La Flèche (founded in 1604), one of the schools which the Jesuits had recently established as part of their intellectual defense of Catholicism against the ideas generated by the Protestant Reformation. Scholarships were available for intelligent but financially poor boys, a practice which enhanced the intellectual level of the student body. It was under this rubric that Marin Mersenne (1588–1648), who would become Descartes's best friend, attended La Flèche. Descartes's father had money, so he was able to take advantage of the option of having a private room. A cousin, Etienne Charlet SJ, was on the staff and became rector in 1608 (later appointed an assistant to the General of the Jesuit order). Descartes entered La Flèche in 1606 and left in 1615 at the age of nineteen. After completing his studies, he qualified in law at the University of Poitiers, but did not work at it. Instead, he served in non-combatant roles in the army of Maurits of Nassau (1567–1625), spent some time traveling, and resided in Paris before moving to The Netherlands in 1628 where he remained for twenty years. Descartes, it should be noted, had the good fortune to have received a comfortable inheritance and hence was never pressed for funds.

In 1649 he accepted an invitation from Queen Christina of Sweden (1626–89) to tutor her in his philosophy. Descartes had always been a very late riser (even at La Flèche), but the Queen nevertheless scheduled their discussions for five in the morning. He caught pneumonia and died on 11 February 1650, a cautionary tale philosophers have always taken seriously! Descartes was a traveler in life and his body was a restless traveler in death. It was first moved to France in 1666 and then transferred to several other locations in Paris. In due course it was reburied (1819) in the chapel of the Sacré Coeur in the church of St. Germain-des-Prés. Along the way, Descartes's skull was removed and replaced with another! There were also problems with Descartes's papers after his death. A friend shipped them from Sweden but the ship carrying the chest containing his manuscripts sank just outside of Paris. His good friend, Claude Clerselier, rescued the chest and then spent days drying out the pages and reassembling them. They included several volumes of correspondence plus the texts of *Treatise on Man* (1662), *The World* (1664), and the *Treatise on the Formation of the Foetus* (1664).

By any standard, Descartes was "present at the creation" of the new science, that mechanization of the world picture to which, among others, Copernicus (1473–1543), Johann Kepler (1571–1630), Galileo (1564–1642), Isaac Beeckman (1588–1637), Marin Mersenne (1588–1648), Robert Boyle (1627–91), Gottfried Wilhelm Leibniz (1646–1716), and Isaac Newton (1643–1727) all contributed in major ways. As a young mathematician, Descartes was instrumental, at a very early age, in the development of analytic geometry. His success in developing an extremely abstract algebraic representation of geometry, thereby minimizing its apparent empirical basis, seems to have deeply affected his thinking about both science and philosophy. His work on inertia and motion contributed directly to the new mechanical physics whose explanatory power did so much to drive Aristotelian science from the scene, although within a generation, Cartesian physics, which did not allow action at a distance, was displaced by Newton's own more powerful account. Descartes also wrote on optics, especially on the law of refraction, despite the fact that Willebrod Snell (1580–1626) had formulated, but not published, the law some years earlier. Descartes tried to discover how blood circulated before William Harvey (1578–1657) produced his own largely definitive solution (1628), at which point Descartes proceeded to defend Harvey's account.

Descartes seems to have acquired his knowledge of science from his wide circle of friends, first in Paris and then in The Netherlands. He matriculated at the University of Franeker in 1629 and a year later in Leiden but we seem to know little about his studies. Franeker is located in Friesland and in Descartes's day was a major university, but its university status was suppressed by Napoleon. Descartes took lodgings initially in the castle of a Catholic family. It provided him with easy access to where he could attend mass.[2] Over the years, Descartes lived in many parts of The Netherlands and established a wide circle of friends (and critics!). Many French people lived for extended periods in The Netherlands (often because of the persecution of the Huguenots) and, generally like English speakers, did not bother to learn the language. This was true even in the 1680s when large numbers of Huguenots were given refuge. Descartes, however, was an exception. Accompanied by a manservant, he was traveling (1621) in a small private craft from Emden en route to West Friesland. The crew, thinking he was a rich foreigner, plotted to rob him. Overhearing them, Descartes immediately drew his sword and told them, in Dutch, that he would kill them if they made any trouble. He thus passed a language test with high stakes![3] In the sixteenth, seventeenth, and for much of the eighteenth century, Latin was the universal language of philosophy, science, and theology. Descartes could read, write, and speak Latin, as could his English, French, and Dutch contemporaries.

The Netherlands was the center of European science in the seventeenth century, and not surprisingly was hence the birthplace of the Enlightenment.[4] The decentralized nature of the Dutch government and the wide diversity in religious opinion made it difficult to suppress the printed or spoken expression of dissident views. Hence a variety of philosophical, scientific, and theological ideas, both orthodox and heterodox, were to be seen and heard. Democratic political ideas as well as arguments on behalf of religious toleration quickly took hold, side by side with the theocratic ideas found among the more orthodox Protestants. Comfortable as he may have been in The Netherlands, he returned to France in 1647 hoping for the recognition which he nevertheless felt had eluded him in The Netherlands. His affairs in Paris did not turn out to his satisfaction: "The innocence of the desert [The Netherlands] from which I came pleases me much more [than Paris] and I do not believe I shall be delayed from returning there in a short time" (letter to Chanut, May 1648). In August 1648 he returned to The Netherlands.

Turning now to more philosophical matters, we are told that Descartes met Isaac Beeckman in 1618 in Breda, The Netherlands. By that time Beeckman had for some years been working on topics which Descartes was beginning to explore. More to the point, they were both looking at the world as mathematical physicists. The sophistication which Beeckman brought to questions in algebra, and geometry, and his analyses of such notions in mechanics (physics) as motion, rest, and falling bodies greatly stimulated Descartes's own thinking. This shift to the use of mathematical models was of course one of the hallmarks of the New Science. Beeckman was generous to a fault to Descartes. He provided ideas, he put his vast scientific knowledge at Descartes's disposal, and corrected likely mistakes. He appreciated that Descartes was a diffi-cult person, but even he may have been surprised to find Descartes, in later years, accusing him of plagiarism.

The strict separation of science from philosophy had not yet developed but the education that Descartes received at La Flèche was in some measure scholastic. That is, the texts and the arguments to which Descartes would have been exposed were in part rooted in the work of such medieval Christian thinkers as Duns Scotus (1265–1308), William of Ockham (1290–1349) and Thomas Aquinas (1225–74). Their theological and philosophical stands were grounded in various ways on Aristotle's views, at least as Aristotle's ideas had been filtered through several centuries of discussion. Islamic philosophers such as Averroes (1126–98) and Avicenna (980–1037) and Jewish thinkers like Moses Maimonides (1138–1204) were also major contributors to the mix.

It is not clear how thoroughly Descartes was immersed in scholastic thought. In a technical sense, scholasticism simply means the "philosophy of the schools," the philosophy which developed in the universities, primarily Paris but also Oxford, in the period from the twelfth through the fifteenth centuries. The philosophy was itself largely a set of variations on the philosophy of Aristotle. Presumably Descartes was acquainted with at least some of the writings of Augustine, Bishop of Hippo (354–430), Duns Scotus,

William of Ockham and Thomas Aquinas. And he clearly was familiar with the writings of the Spanish Jesuit, Francisco Suárez (1548–1617), often described as the last of the scholastics.

The primary focus of Descartes's philosophy was not scholastic in nature. Instead, he was influenced by scientific concerns of the New Science and the threats to that science posed by scepticism. The principle literary source for scepticism as a systematic philosophy is Sextus Empiricus. But before we turn to Sextus Empiricus and the arguments of the Pyrrhonians, a few other historical details are in order. Although manuscripts of Sextus's writing must have been stored in one or another of the libraries in the Mediterranean area including those in Byzantium, his views made little impact on the major figures of the medieval period. They were interested in problems of knowledge and certitude, the nature of the world, and the processes whereby we acquire concepts. But they were not troubled by the sorts of doubts about knowledge which were later to haunt sixteenth- and seventeenth-century philosophers and theologians. However, half a millennium earlier, Augustine did deal explicitly with sceptical problems. Since he was one of the most important Fathers of the Latin Church, his discussions were read in the middle ages. And there is every reason to think that Descartes read portions of Augustine. He admits as much in some of his comments. Augustine, unlike the medievals, was well acquainted with one of the classical sources for scepticism, the *Academica* (45 BC) of Cicero (106–43 BC). While he was apparently not familiar with the much more rigorous arguments of Sextus, he was very concerned to provide some sort of refutation of Academic scepticism. To that end we find in a number of places passages which sound Cartesian, that is they sound a bit like Descartes's famous *cogito ergo sum* (I think therefore I am) – which will be discussed below. In his *City of God*, Augustine writes: "If the [sceptics] say 'what if you are mistaken?' well, if I am mistaken, I am. For if one does not exist, he can by no means be mistaken" (Bk XI, ch. 26). Somewhat similar points are made in, e.g., *On the free will* (Bk II, ch. iii, § 7), and in his *Treatise on the holy trinity* (Bk XV, ch. xii, § 23).

It was only, however, at the end of the medieval period and the emergence of the Renaissance that genuinely sceptical difficulties began to emerge. One reason may have been that during the high middle ages, a decision procedure was built into the Church. Councils plus the Pope could deal with problems. Perhaps as Jewish and Islamic questions began to occupy the minds of scholars, debates began which were not totally enclosed by Christian thinking. Throughout the middle ages, at the very least from the time of the First Crusade (1096), the Church increased its pressure on Jews, culminating in the activities of the Inquisition, especially in Spain, in the fifteenth century. If the suppression of Jews and Moslems was to succeed, knowledge of their doctrines had to be obtained. Yet knowledge of their ideas and customs could prove dangerous to Catholic orthodoxy. Those dangers were to materialize in subsequent years.

The decline in the role of the scholastics went hand in hand with the intellectual excitement of the Renaissance, the recovery of Greek and Latin learning thanks to such scholars as Erasmus of Rotterdam (1467–1536) and the development of the New Humanism by a range of scholars, such as Marsilio Ficino (1433–99), who, like many Florentines, much preferred Plato to Aristotle, and who were open to Arabic and Jewish (especially Kabbalistic) learning. There were other major figures such as Savonarola (1452–98), who was executed by the Church. He was in turn an influence on John Pico della Mirandola (1463–94) and his nephew John Francis Pico della Mirandola (1469–1533). All three took seriously the arguments of the Greek sceptic, Sextus Empiricus (fl. 2nd century AD). The goal of their reintroduction of Sextus Empiricus and his Pyrrhonism, as that form of scepticism was known, seems to have been primarily religious. If one used the arguments of Sextus properly, one could cleanse the mind of human pride and arrogance. Such a cleansed mind would then be open to God's installation of the Christian faith without the many stumbling blocks which philosophical talk traditionally introduced. Their goal was thus to use scepticism to prepare one for the acceptance of the Christian faith, but a faith unsullied by philosophical considerations. Most philosophers and theologians who utilized Pyrrhonism in the centuries that followed were not interested in the goal Pyrrho (about 360–270 BC) set for his movement (that is putting things too dogmatically! He would not have agreed that he was founding anything!), namely, a way of life. Those who proposed *fideism*, that is the appeal to pure faith, took Pyrrhonism solely as a preparation for faith, not something that was good in itself, and certainly not as a way of life. Savonarola and the Picos were proposing a route via Pyrrhonism to the Christian way of life.

A relatively small number of philosophers had been acquainted with Sextus through manuscript sources in, e.g., the fifteenth century but, as Luciano Floridi has been establishing in his recent work, more than had previously been known. The difficulty in gauging Sextus's influence in the (early) Renaissance is that while he affected religious concerns in a quiet way, there was a lack of interest in the anti-theory of knowledge function of Pyrrhonian arguments.[5] The dramatic quality of Sextus's influence came only in the second half of the sixteenth century when his arguments were directly applied to claims to knowledge in the context of scientific matters. Cicero's *Academica* also gradually became better known. Sceptical ideas and arguments were much more widely disseminated with the publication of the writings of Sextus in Latin translation in 1562 and 1569. A less technical source – and one written in French – was Michel de Montaigne (1533–92). His father was Catholic but his mother was from a Jewish "New Christian" family, i.e. from a Jewish family which had been (usually forcibly) converted to Catholicism under the Inquisition. She, like a number of New Christians who managed to leave Spain or Portugal, became a Protestant. The author of scores of essays and still ranked as a world-class literary figure, the longest of Montaigne's many essays was on sceptical themes. One theme was the application of sceptical arguments to perceptual and knowledge claims. Another was the use of Pyrrhonism in the context of religious faith, specifically on the use, already noted, of scepticism as both a bulwark against the role of reason in religion and also as a defense of pure faith, matters which increased in importance as the Reformation's impact spread across Europe. This essay, *The Apology for Raymond Sebond* (1580 ff), wraps up the many technical arguments of Sextus in a delightful collection of extraordinarily lively and amusing tales. He culled many stories from classical sources about the intelligence and morality of animals, usually by way of contrast with human behavior. The animals generally come out ahead! Sextus Empiricus and Pyrrhonism appear in the text. And on the ceiling of his Library, some fifty-seven sayings or sentences are etched into the beams. Most (19) are from the Bible; the next largest number (12) are from Sextus Empiricus. And as noted, in the text of the *Apology*, Montaigne uses Pyrrhonism in support of religion:

> [Pyrrhonism] presents man naked and empty, acknowledging his natural weakness, fit to receive from above some outside power; stripped of human knowledge, and all the more apt to lodge divine knowledge in himself, annihilating his judgment to make more room for faith ... [One thus becomes] humble, obedient, teachable, zealous; a sworn enemy of heresy ... He is a blank tablet prepared to take from the finger of God such forms as he shall be pleased to engrave on it.

About Aristotle, he says: "The god of scholastic knowledge is Aristotle; it is a religious matter to discuss any of his ordinances." Nor is he happy about the Academic sceptics and their acceptance of probable judgments. He presents an objection which the ancient Pyrrhonians had made: "How can they [the Academic sceptics] let themselves be inclined toward the likeness of truth, if they know not the truth?" All of the sceptical arguments against claims to truth can, Montaigne believed, be revised to be directed against claims to be "probable." But his favorite arguments are to notice conflict cases where a criterion is called for in order to decide between, say, one sense and another, or between sense and reason. Following Sextus (*Outlines of Pyrrhonism*, II, vii, 75), he also gives currency to a problem which not only carried forward to Descartes, but from Descartes on to Bayle and Berkeley. He poses a fundamental challenge to theories that speak of a resemblance between our perceptions and objects in the world.

> The conception and semblance we form is not of the object, but only of the impression and effect made on the sense; which impression and the object are different things ... As for saying that the impressions of the senses convey to the soul the quality of the foreign objects by resemblance, how can the soul and understanding make

sure of this resemblance, having of itself no communication with foreign objects? Just as a man who does not know Socrates, seeing his portrait, cannot say that it resembles him.

Further, how does one decide such matters as which senses should have priority over others, what is the criterion in such cases, or who can then serve as the judge in disputes, etc. He rehearses the traditional Pyrrhonian questions about "deceptions" as when one has the report of one sense apparently in conflict with another. Although a stick in water appears bent when it crosses the surface, if our hand holds the stick at the same time, it feels straight. These and similar apparent anomalies suggest that given the existence of such so-called "variations in sense experience" it seems impossible to get behind appearances to locate the real things. He also challenges the role of reason, thereby casting doubts not only on the senses but also on the soundness of reason and on science and geometry. And of course appeals to the criterion argument are omnipresent, like traps for the unwary. A generation or so later, i.e. by Descartes's time, the intellectual atmosphere was saturated with sceptical arguments.

Writers in the sixteenth, seventeenth and eighteenth centuries were not inclined to document their sources. Their texts seldom contain many footnotes. But nevertheless both Montaigne, and his adopted son, Canon Pierre Charron (1541–1603), were significant influences on Descartes and are mentioned by him. Charron produced a systematic version of Montaigne's sceptical arguments and much enhanced the importance of his scepticism and his reliance on pure faith in matters of religion as well as his scepticism with regard both to reason and sense experience. His *De la sagesse* ["Wisdom"] (1601) was a widely read and frequently reprinted book. However, the *intellectual* turmoil which characterized the sixteenth century was not merely a function of the forces unleashed by the Renaissance but more importantly, as Montaigne maintained, by the Protestant Reformation. Nevertheless, Montaigne's importance for the history of modern philosophy can hardly be over-estimated. He set the stage for developments in seventeenth-century philosophy. He was not only a direct influence on Descartes, but he presented the scepticism of Sextus not simply as part of a preparation for faith, but also – and this proved of crucial importance – as a systematic challenge to philosophy and science.

It is a mistake to think that the Protestants who had to take up the challenge of scepticism were especially anti-scholastic. Their own writings were often dominated by scholastic philosophical ideas and methods even as they attacked the Catholic Church. This should not surprise us. Universities are very conservative institutions and moves away from scholasticism came very slowly, as Descartes was to discover. The excitement which the Reformation caused arose from something quite distinct. La Flèche had been founded not to be a center of scholastic thought nor to defend medieval ideas but to prepare the young intellectuals they successfully recruited to do battle on behalf of the Church. In other words, colleges (like La Flèche) set up as components of the so-called Counter-Reformation took as their task the equipping of their students with the intellectual tools, rhetorical skills, and acquaintance with the arguments of their opponents which would enable Catholicism to triumph over the Protestants.

The arguments of the Reformers, particularly Martin Luther (1483–1546) and John Calvin (1509–64) challenged the very foundations of the Catholic Church by posing the question: which Church is the True Church? The question had been raised explicitly or implicitly before, but those who had raised it in the past were either marginalized or eliminated. This time, the arguments of the Reformers were taken seriously. The Protestants threw down this challenge: the Roman Church claims to be the arbiter of Holy Scripture and the interpreter of the Christian tradition. By what right does the Church claim its authority as ultimate arbiter? Answer: by its appeal to Holy Scripture. But circular reasoning cannot be avoided, according to the Protestants, since the Church's authority to interpret Holy Scripture is based on its own interpretation of Scripture.

The position of the Reformers had its own problems since it accorded primacy to the words of Scripture as reflected in each individual's private conscience. An obvious problem, one which surfaced almost immediately, is how to resolve disputes among the faithful. The primary philosophical issue generated by the Reformation is one which has tormented philosophers from that time onward: do we have a defensible criterion of truth? And we must have a criterion if we are to specify which Church is the True Church. The so-called criterion problem was not a major consideration among the medievals. Aristotle was unsympathetic to sceptical questions and within the medieval world, the Church already had its traditional means for mediating and resolving conflicts. But once the Church's authority was effectively brought into question by the Reformation, arguments to defend or undermine criteria came to the fore. And a perfect handbook of arguments was found in the texts of Sextus. His methodology was geared precisely to expose the difficulties in establishing a criterion, any criterion.

For those who, like Richard Popkin (1923–), see scepticism at the very core of the rise of modern philosophy, two elements were decisive. The Protestant Reformation challenged the presuppositions, the very foundations, of the Christian worldview. But something else was required. And as Popkin sees it, that was provided by Sextus. It was in Sextus and his Pyrrhonism, rather than the Academic sceptics, that one met with systematic arguments against the criterion, arguments which had no parallel in Cicero. It was Sextus's Pyrrhonian challenge to the criterion which gave disruptive power to the arguments of the Reformers and their Catholic opponents and thereby gave rise, in large measure, to the intellectual crisis of the seventeenth century and hence to the development, as in the work of Descartes, of a "modern" philosophy which sought to come to grips, in one way or another, with the crisis. The Picos and their comrades did not have to cope with the Reformation. They were less worried about achieving philosophical or scientific truths than they were about religious considerations. It is also true that not every philosopher in the late sixteenth- and early seventeenth-centuries was taken up with the crisis or sought to "refute" the sceptics. Some were satisfied with seeking a *modus vivendi* and were content with probabilities rather than certainties.

Regarding the criterion, Sextus held that the claim that a proposition is true requires that the proposition be judged to be true in accordance with a criterion. The difficulty seems to be insurmountable: the criterion against which we measure that something is true must *itself* be known to be true, which means that one already needs to know what is true in order to specify the criterion, but one needs a criterion in order to know what is true. Thus one appears to be faced with circular reasoning. Sextus polishes and hones these and similar arguments. For example, to settle a dispute over perceptual data, a judge is required. That requires someone who is not a party to the dispute. But every human is a party to this dispute. The arguments of the sceptics are often directed at criteria for distinguishing between what *appears* and what we claim is *real*, and are thus readily translatable from examining putative claims to knowledge in matters of Christian religious controversy. More generally, Sextus discusses at length problems in logic, mathematics, grammar, physics, and ethics and his techniques were quickly employed in religious polemics.

The original goal of the sceptical methodology in its Pyrrhonian form is to bring one to "a state of mental suspense and next to a state of 'unperturbedness' or quietude."[6] The sceptic seeks release from, so-to-speak, the mental cramps induced by dogmatic ideas. But the "arguments," and Sextus is very careful not to be dogmatic about the certainty of his arguments or even their persuasive powers, are extendable beyond his own text. That is why his texts constitute a mine of devices capable of undermining the (often dogmatic) claims of one's opponents. The person who has advanced a so-called dogmatic position has a stake in his or her own arguments and the arguments of the sceptic are parasitic upon them. If the sceptic picks apart one's own argument, if the sceptic finds a flaw in one's own argument, it is faint comfort to respond by saying: "I don't have to take your refutations of my position seriously because you refuse to assert the truth of your own arguments."

The Catholics, who were only too happy to promulgate the sceptical arguments of Sextus Empiricus, initially had the advantage. After all, the Protestants were trying to persuade Catholics to leave their traditional Church because of the errors said to infest it and to join a new Church, one which claimed to be True. Sceptical methodology was the perfect antidote. To join a *new* Church one should first know it to be the True Church lest one jeopardize one's salvation, as Montaigne (among others) pointed out. The trouble was that by the middle of the second half of the sixteenth century all parties found that they could play the sceptical game. By what criteria can we decide which book is the Bible, which interpretation of a text is correct, which person is the Pope, etc.? For example, one might grant for the sake of the argument that the Pope is infallible, but one would oneself have to be infallible to know with certainty which person is the infallible Pope. Conclusion: the only person who knows with certainty which person is the Pope is the Pope.[7] The Protestants, in turn, might claim that the true rule of faith is Scripture, but that most crucial rule, on which their religion rests, does not itself occur in Scripture! All parties to the religious disputes soon realized that attacks on one's opponents could be turned against one's self, except that the combatants often believed their own bases to be grounded not on rational principles but instead on faith and hence not amenable to sceptical attack. In the meantime, the many arguments of Sextus were available for all to see – and to use.

To sum up, I have provided some of the historical background and the philosopical and religious importance of ideas of the great sceptics. I have attributed special influence and importance to Montaigne as well as to the Reformation. These two factors set the stage, so to speak, for the arrival of Descartes on the scene. I shall now show how these ideas became a major topic for Descartes as he assumed the role of slayer of scepticism.

"On many occasions I have in sleep been deceived"

There is no reason to doubt that Descartes was exposed at least to some medieval scholastic thought when he was a student at La Flèche, but several of his teachers were primarily fierce polemicists, keen of wit and sharp of tongue – ever prepared to do battle with their Protestant opponents. Given the purpose for which La Flèche had been founded a few years before Descartes became a student, given the polemical atmosphere, given the widespread use of the arguments of the sceptics, it is hardly surprising that Descartes took scepticism seriously and, like his friend Mersenne, devoted years to refuting it. Contemporaries may have found sceptical arguments a source of fun and intellectual pleasure, but Descartes was never amused. He saw scepticism as a menace, a menace which could not be constrained within the limits of theological/religious debate. Both Protestants and Catholics who engaged in the wars over the True religion and who utilized the arguments of Sextus Empiricus did not take seriously the risk that the arguments could be applied to their own religious beliefs. Sceptical arguments enabled one to cleanse one's psyche of philosophical clap-trap so as to stand naked before God and thus be in a position to receive God's Word. They took their religious beliefs to be grounded in a faith purely God-given and hence not to be affected by sceptical arguments. But unlike those who employed scepticism in the interests of their religious concerns, Descartes understood that Pyrrhonism had the power not simply to challenge one's religious opponents, it had the terrible power to be able to undermine all science and all claims to knowledge. That is why he believed it had to be refuted.

Descartes begins his attack on scepticism in his two best-known philosophical treatises, first, a text written in French so as to be available to non-specialists, the *Discourse on the Method of Rightly Conducting one's Reason and Seeking the Truth in the Sciences* (1637) usually shortened to the *Discourse*, and, written in Latin, his *Meditations on First Philosophy; in which the existence of God and the distinction between the human soul and the body are demonstrated* (1641), usually referred to simply as the *Meditations*. Although it has long been noted that Descartes does not appear to have been troubled in his own intellectual life by sceptical problems, we know that as early as 1629 he reacted strongly to attempts to attack even Aristotelian science if one had nothing better to put in its place.

In 1637 Descartes published the *Discourse* together with three other works: his *Optics*, *Geometry*, and *Meteorology*. In Part II of the *Discourse*, he tells us that having some leisure on his hands, while in Germany, and having no attractive diversions, he "remained the whole day shut up alone in a stove-heated room," and drafted the set of reflections which constitute the *Discourse* (HR I, 87; AT vi, 11). His first biographer, Adrien Baillet (1649–1706), on the basis of material now lost, tells us that Descartes also had three dreams – dreams which even Sigmund Freud (1856–1939) failed satisfactorily to unravel! But the story of the dreams and the "stove–heated room" give a rich romantic flavor to the opening of the *Discourse*. Descartes soon puts aside the romantic style and returns to his search for truth. He says:

> But as regards all the opinions which up to this time I had embraced, I thought I could not do better than endeavour once for all to sweep them completely away, so that they might later on be replaced, either by others which were better, or by the same, when I had made them conform to the uniformity of a rational scheme. And I firmly believed that by this means I should succeed in directing my life much better than if I had only built on old foundations, and relied on

principles which I allowed myself to be in youth persuaded without having inquired into their truth. (HR I, 89; AT vi, 13–14)

To this radical proposal he adds:

> The simple resolve to strip oneself of all opinions and beliefs formerly received is not to be regarded as an example that each man should follow, and the world may be said to be mainly composed of two classes of minds neither of which could prudently adopt it. There are those who, believing themselves to be cleverer than they are, cannot restrain themselves from being precipitate in judgment and have not sufficient patience to arrange their thoughts in proper order; hence, once a man of this description had taken the liberty of doubting the principles he formerly accepted, and had deviated from the beaten track, he would never be able to maintain the path which must be followed to reach the appointed end more quickly, and he would hence remain wandering astray all through his life. (HR I, 90; AT vi, 15)

He includes a point of view which would hardly endear him to people in authority: "I could not ... put my finger on a single person whose opinions seemed preferable to those of others, and I found that I was, so to speak, constrained myself to undertake the direction of my procedure" (HR I, 91; AT vi, 16).

It is in Part III of the *Discourse* that Descartes tells us that he formed a provisional code of morals while in the process of constructing a sound foundation for knowledge:

> The first [maxim] was to obey the laws and customs of my country, adhering constantly to the religion in which by God's grace I had been instructed since my childhood, and in all other things directing my conduct by opinions the most moderate in nature, and the farthest removed from excess in all those which are commonly received and acted on by the most judicious of those with whom I might come in contact. (HR I, 95; AT vi, 23)

There are at least three methodological themes in the *Discourse*.

    1. Descartes seeks a route to the truth. And his route is definitely not by appealing to authorities of any sort. This anti-authoritarian streak in Descartes can be read as pure

arrogance, or as a pre-emptive strike against those who would cast his ideas into the bottomless pit of classical and scholastic debates, or as reflecting his hostility towards clerical censorship. Thus he says that he will "accept nothing as true which I did not clearly recognize to be so … and to accept [in my judgments] nothing more than what was presented to my mind so clearly and distinctly that I could have no occasion to doubt it" (Part II, HR I, 92; AT vi, 18). What he means by clear and distinct, complex notions that play a crucial role in the argument of the *Meditations*, will be discussed below.

2. In Part II, Descartes recommends that we divide up each of our difficulties into "as many parts as possible." And then we should proceed from the most simple, step-by-step, to the most complicated. And last, "in all cases to make enumerations so complete and reviews so general that I should be certain of having omitted nothing." The model for Descartes's methodology was, clearly, that of mathematics. With small steps and constant checking one could be *relatively* confident about one's results.

3. How does one escape the errors one makes and the doubts which pursue one? We can be deceived "even concerning the simplest matters of geometry." Worse, "since all the same thoughts and conceptions which we have while awake may also come to us in sleep … I resolved to assume that everything that ever entered into my mind was no more true than the illusions of my dreams" (Part IV, HR I, 101; AT vi, 32). This puzzle, so famous (or infamous) that it is simply called the "dream problem," has a long history. It is of course found in Sextus Empiricus, e.g. at *Outlines of Pyrrhonism* (I, 100, 113)[8] and *Against the Mathematicians* (VII, 60–64), but also in Plato (*Theaetetus* [158 B–C]) and Aristotle (*Metaphysics*, 1011a7 ff).

Descartes's formulation in the *Meditations* is perhaps more crisp than the version he presents in the *Discourse*:

At this moment it does indeed seem to me that it is with eyes wide awake that I am looking at this paper; that this head which I move is not asleep, that it is deliberately and of set purpose that I extend my hand and perceive it; what happens in sleep does not appear so clear nor so distinct as does all this. But in thinking over this I remind myself that *on many occasions I have in sleep been deceived* by similar illusions, and in dwelling carefully on this reflection I see so manifestly that there are no certain indications by which we may clearly distinguish wakefulness from sleep that I am lost in astonishment. And my astonishment is such that it is almost capable of persuading me that I now dream. (Med. I, HR I, 146; AT vi, 19; my emphasis)

After pondering the earlier version of the dream problem formulated in the *Discourse*, Descartes begins to contemplate escaping from it rather than "solving" it. He writes:

Immediately afterwards I noticed that whilst I thus wished to think all things false, it was absolutely essential that the "I" who thought this should be somewhat, and remarking that this truth "*I think, therefore I am*" was so certain and so assured that all the most extravagant suppositions brought forward by the sceptics were incapable of shaking it, I came to the conclusion that I could receive it without scruple as the first principle of the Philosophy for which I was seeking.[9]

The principle, "I think therefore I am," reads in Latin: *cogito ergo sum*, which is why it is generally shortened in citations to "*cogito*." Descartes then notes that the marks of its truth are its clarity and distinctness and that whatever we conceive clearly and distinctly is true. Descartes next seeks to show how this connects with the existence of God, a matter he takes up in detail in the *Meditations*. One major topic which is discussed in the *Discourse* but not the *Meditations* is the linguistic ability of humans.

Descartes believes that there is a fundamental difference between humans and animals. The difference is not rooted in a lack of organs but rather in a non-mechanical feature of humankind. We, unlike animals, are composed of two substances – minds whose essence is to think and in which our bodies play no part, and bodies, which are extended portions of matter. What are the marks of the distinction between humans and animals?

[Animals] could never use speech or other signs as we do when placing our thoughts on record for the benefit of others. For we can easily understand a machine's being constituted so that it can utter words, and even emit some responses to action on it of a corporeal [bodily] kind ... for instance, if it is touched in a particular part it may ask what we wish to say to it; if in another part it may exclaim that it is being hurt ... But it never happens that it arranges its speech in various ways, in order to reply appropriately to everything that may be said in its presence, as even the lowest type of man can do ... (HR I, 116; AT vi, 56–57)

Some ancient Greek philosophers had already noted that the human mind had the remarkable capacity of being able to "think the thing that is not." We can think and talk about the future and the past, we can imagine events happening differently. We need not be occupied with what is in front of our noses, i.e., with our immediate environment. We can talk, or not talk as the case may be, with our friends. And we can talk about virtually anything!

Noam Chomsky (1928–), who has fired up the "machines of war" by reminding us of Descartes's views, formulates Descartes's position this way:

Man has a species-specific capacity, a unique type of intellectual organization which cannot be attributed to peripheral organs or related to general intelligence and which manifests itself in what we may refer to as the "creative aspect" of ordinary language use – its property of being both unbounded in scope and stimulus-free. Thus Descartes maintains that language is available for the free expression of thought or for appropriate response in any new context and is undetermined by any fixed association of utterances to external stimuli or physiological states (identifiable in any noncircular fashion).

Chomsky holds that it is the "appropriateness" of our responses, as Descartes put it, that is beyond the limits of "mechanical explanation." Moreover, "Modern studies of animal communication so far offer no counterevidence to the Cartesian assumption that human language is based on an entirely distinct principle."[10]

There are two factors which have driven the return to innate ideas. First is what is called "the argument from the poverty of the stimulus".[11] As children we very quickly develop a rich facility with language on the basis of extremely limited data. Children learn to do such things with language as how to form questions, how to form passives, etc., without any "teaching." Moreover, children are able to understand sentences which they have never heard before. Indeed, most of what they say and what they hear has not been said before. Conclusion: our language skills are not a product of input from the world via induction and repetition. Our mind/brain is pre-structured to process the language we hear and see. Mathematics is another area in which the appeal to the "poverty of the stimulus" also holds. Like language, our rich knowledge of mathematics reaches far beyond such data as we may encounter. In fact, it is hard to imagine why people of an empiricist persuasion ever thought (and some still think) that on the basis of a *blank tablet*, we could peel off, so to speak, words and numbers from the world we encounter. Second, there is the creative activity with language which Descartes, as noted, took to be a uniquely human capacity. Neither can be handled within a purely empiricist framework.

Descartes introduces a second substance, i.e. mind or spirit, within which all mental phenomena are located, because he could not explain the language faculty within the science of mechanics he had at his disposal. That appeal to a second substance has not been much admired by a majority of philosophers and scientists over the next several centuries. In the twentieth century psychologists and philosophers sought and in the twenty-first, continue to seek to establish that human and animal behavior are to be located along a continuum. They are not inclined to take seriously our capacity to "think the thing that is not." And they are opposed to dualism, i.e. the thesis that we are composed of two substances. This opposition often seems to arise because of anti-religious feelings. Some people seem to think that were mind–body dualism true, we should run quickly to the nearest monastery or nunnery!

Several points are lost in the emotions generated by talk about dualism. First, Descartes introduced dualism for a perfectly good scientific reason. He needed to find a place for activities which could not be encompassed by the physics (contact mechanics) available to him. There was no room for mental events within that scientific model. Second, dualism does not figure in the traditional Christian creeds. There the core stated belief is in the *resurrection of the body*. Third, there is nothing new in the suggestion that our minds are distinct from and act independently of our bodies. A number of very "orthodox" medieval theologians subscribe to that. Fourth, the real basis for hostility towards dualism, and indeed, towards Descartes, is what I shall call ideological.

The Cartesian revolution may begin with the attempt to refute scepticism and to construct a foundation for his mathematical worldview, but its most lasting impact has been in constructing nothing less than a fundamentally new account of human nature. In this respect, Descartes successfully initiates a war between what have come to be known as the rationalist and the empiricist doctrines of human nature. It is an exciting war, as debates about human nature always are, and we are still in its midst. As we shall see, it is a war with many ramifications from teaching and learning, sexism and racism, the roles of history versus nature, individuals versus communities, from control of populations to political issues more generally. Descartes's few lines on language in Part V of his *Discourse*, combined with his defense of dualism, had the effect of opening Pandora's box.

Descartes began to be *the philosopher philosophers love to hate* while he still lived in The Netherlands. He may have chosen The Netherlands as a place to live (and he lived there for twenty years) because he believed he would be less disturbed than he might be in France. And, despite the conflicts he had with the philosophers and theologians at Utrecht and Leiden, he probably had less trouble there than he would have had in Paris. But he was a prickly sort of person, very concerned that he receive the respect he felt he deserved. He crossed swords not only with those he felt were out to damage his reputation and to place his peace in various communities at risk, but even with those who tried to agree with him and who in every respect wished him well. He was dismayed when his daughter Francine, baptized a Protestant, died as a child. He is reported to have supported the mother. Yet he managed to antagonize even so loyal a friend as Beeckman. One of their arguments concerned the transmission of light. Beeckman argued that if something was corporeal, its transmission would take time. Descartes held that light's transmission was instantaneous. Descartes was forever complaining to Mersenne about the treatment he received at the hands of scientists (not surprising if one recalls that he accused his friend and "teacher" Beeckman of plagiarism). At the end of the *Discourse* Descartes had asked for criticisms from his readers.

> I do not wish to anticipate the judgment of any one by myself speaking of my writings; but I shall be very glad if they will examine them. And in order that they may have the better opportunity of so doing, I beg all those who have any objections to offer to take the trouble of sending them to my publishers, so that, being made aware of them, I may try at the same time to subjoin my reply. By this means, the reader, seeing objections and reply at the same time, will the more easily judge of the truth; for I do not promise in any instance to make lengthy replies, but just to avow my errors very frankly if I am convinced of them; or, if I cannot perceive them, to say simply what I think requisite for the defence of the matters I have written, without adding the exposition of any new matter, so that I may not be endlessly engaged in passing from one side to the other. (HR I, 128; AT vi, 75–76)

Descartes was not, however, pleased with the criticisms he received. "The French mathematicians who criticized his *Geometry* were dismissed as 'two or three flies' ... Roberval is described as 'less than a rational animal' ... Pierre Petit as a 'little dog' ... Hobbes as 'extremely contemptible' ... Jean de Beaugrand's letters are only good to be used as [in effect] 'toilet paper'."

The great mathematician Pierre Fermat (1601–65) also responded to Descartes's request. He drew attention to some difficulties in the *Optics*. Descartes responded with elegance by describing Fermat's comments as "shit."[12]

This chapter has described some of the reasons Descartes came under attack. Still, none of these factors explains the waves of hostility towards Descartes which swept across the intellectual landscape in the twentieth century and which continue to do so today.

"Some evil genius (not less powerful than deceitful) has employed his whole energies in deceiving me"

The *Meditations* is both the primary target for the opponents of Descartes as well as being the primary source for our knowledge of his philosophy. Published in 1641, the text is more systematically written than the *Discourse*, although like the *Discourse*, it is divided into six parts (Meditations). Moreover, Descartes's most loyal and best friend, Marin Mersenne – who had been a few years his senior at La Flèche – circulated the text among a number of scholars. Mersenne joined the Order of the Minims and became a priest in 1613. Aside from being a close friend of Descartes, Mersenne was also a serious scientist and philosopher in his own right. He wrote a huge book attacking the sceptics (*La verité des sciences contre les septiques ou Pyrrhoniens* [1625]). While Sextus's arguments might be irrefutable, it was nevertheless possible to accrue vast amounts of useful information and thus pragmatically to deter the impact of scepticism. It is said that he became a "one man society for the advancement of science." Scientists and philosophers left copies of their work with him so that others might stop by at his monastic cell and study them. Six of his acquaintances prepared criticisms of the *Meditations* and Descartes in turn responded to them. So one speaks of the *Objections and Replies*. Not often have philosophers and scientists exposed themselves to such penetrating and often hostile questions. But they enabled Descartes to clarify and expand upon his views. And they help us to understand his ideas, and of course they sometimes add complications and confusion.

In the *Discourse* Descartes immediately sets about his philosophical tasks. Although written only three or four years later, the *Meditations* begins in a totally different fashion. It begins with a dedication: *To those most learned and most illustrious men, the Dean and Doctors of the Sacred Faculty of Theology of Paris.* This is followed by several pages in which Descartes is clearly seeking the support and, so to speak, the blessing of the members of the Faculty, a faculty which was seen by many to be the supreme arbiter of religious questions for the entire (i.e. the French!) Catholic Church.

> I have always considered that the two questions respecting God and the Soul, were the chief of those that ought to be demonstrated by philosophical rather than theological argument ... And as regards the soul, although many have considered that it is not easy to know its nature, and some have even dared to say that human reasons have convinced us that it would perish with the body, and that faith alone could believe the contrary, nevertheless, inasmuch as the Lateran Council held under Leo X (in the eighth session) condemns these tenets, and as Leo expressly ordains Christian philosophers to refute their arguments and to employ all their powers in making known the truth, I have ventured in this treatise to undertake the same task. (HR I, 133–134; AT vii, 1–3)

Descartes states that he hopes the Faculty will "take them [the *Meditations*] under [its] protection." After the condemnation of Galileo (1633) Descartes suppressed his own heliocentric views. Certainly his hope for approval from the Church was disappointed. He was soon severely criticized by both Catholic and Protestant theologians and his writings were later placed on the Church's *Index of Prohibited Books*. In addition to this remarkable letter of dedication, Descartes wrote a multi-page *Synopsis* of the *Meditations*. It will be discussed below. In a discussion (1648) with his young friend, Frans Burman (1628–79), Descartes's real sentiments about theology were made clear. He says to Burman that theology rests on revealed truths and should not be subjected to philosophical criticism. But because the monks did precisely that, they are responsible for generating all the sects and heresies. Their "scholastic theology should above all be destroyed [*détruire*] ... [in the meantime] the theologians hardly do anything else than slander [one another]."[13]

In the first *Meditation* Descartes presents several sceptical problems which he must then spend the other five "solving." It will, he says at the very outset, be enough for him to reject as false anything in which he finds a ground for doubt. First of all, he notes that the "senses occasionally deceive us." Sextus and Montaigne both give all sorts of "reasons" for doubting the veracity of our sense experience. As in the *Discourse*, Descartes deals only with one, again, the so-called "dream problem." How do we distinguish our dreams from our waking experience? Are there any marks whereby we can be certain that we are not dreaming? After all, if there were a certified and true criterion, we would not have nightmares. We could just see, in effect, what channel we were tuned into – dream or waking experience. But we can't. Since Descartes is recommending that we should reject as false that which we can doubt, sensory experience is not a reliable guide to knowledge. Philosophers have puzzled about the dream problem since Plato's time. The most insightful (and amusing) discussion with which I am acquainted is by O. K. Bouwsma.[14] Briefly, Bouwsma argues that for there to be a deception, there must be a way of understanding how the deceptive "trick" is played. But there isn't in the case of dreams and hence the term deception is misapplied. Descartes's nightmare problem, however, remains.

Descartes notices that in the dream context there is something special about arithmetic and geometry, namely that "whether I am awake or asleep, two and three together always form five, and the square can never have more than four sides" (HR I, 147; AT vii, 20). A mathematical problem solved in a dream is nevertheless a mathematical problem solved. Physics, on the other hand, is in a different category because it deals with "composite" entities, ones in which sensory material is mixed with mathematical concepts and it is hence, like astronomy and medicine, subject to the dream problem.

The second sceptical element Descartes introduces usually goes under the label the "demon problem." There have often been theologians who seek to show the absolute power and preeminence of God, and who see any attempt to restrict God to what is logically true as an invasion of his power and a display of human pride. These philosophers and theologians have often been in the tradition of William of Ockham. Descartes seems to be aware of that tradition and to be willing to explore the full range of God's omnipotence. There is no evidence, however, that Descartes's God would violate the laws of logic. God sets them up (at will) but cannot then violate them. What Descartes does say (in a letter to Mersenne 27 May 1630 [AT i, 152]) is that:

> You ask also what necessitated God to create these [eternal] truths; and I reply that he was free to make it not true that all the radii of the circle are equal – just as free as he was not to create the world. And it is certain that these truths are no more necessarily attached to his essence than are other created things.[15]

But the "demon deceiver" poses a troubling puzzle. Thus where the dream problem is used to raise sceptical doubts about evidence said to be derived from sense experience, the demon deceiver which Descartes postulates can apparently undermine arithmetic and geometry and even logic itself. "At the end I feel constrained to confess that there is nothing at all that I formerly believed to be true, of which I cannot in some measure doubt" (HR I, 147–148; AT vii, 22). This is how Descartes formulates the demon problem:

> I shall then suppose, not that God who is supremely good and the fountain of truth, but some evil genius not less powerful than deceitful, has employed his whole energies in deceiving me … I shall remain obstinately attached to this idea, and if by this means it is not in my power to arrive at the knowledge of any truth, I may at least do what is in my power [i.e. suspend my judgment], and with firm purpose avoid giving credence to any false thing, or being imposed upon by this arch deceiver, however powerful and deceptive he may be. (HR I, 148; AT vii, 22–23)

The demon deceiver is not a part of any traditional sceptical methodology. In fact, in his Reply to the seventh set of Objections to the *Meditations*, Descartes says he has insisted that this "supreme kind of doubt ... is metaphysical, hyperbolical and not to be transferred to the sphere of the practical needs of life by any means" (HR II, 266; AT vii, 460). The traditional Greek sceptics, those in the Pyrrhonian tradition of Sextus Empiricus, would be perplexed by Descartes's use of this argument as well as by his apparent attempt to circumscribe its use. It is hard to see how it would help one reach the Pyrrhonian goal of a state of "mental quietude." On the contrary, it seems calculated to induce anxiety and frustration. There is, it should be noted, no evidence that Descartes himself was especially troubled by sceptical anxieties. While it is true that prior to 1637 Descartes appears to display little interest in purely sceptical problems, he was always concerned with matters of certainty and methods for achieving it. And yet, starting with 1637 there is a genuine revolution in his thought. At the very least, he had come to appreciate the risks to science which scepticism could create. In the second *Meditation* he writes:

> Archimedes, in order that he might draw the terrestrial globe out of its place, and transport it elsewhere, demanded only that one point should be fixed and immovable; in the same way I shall have the right to conceive high hopes if I am happy enough to discover one thing only which is certain and indubitable. (HR I, 149; AT vii, 24)

He then adds a most remarkable claim:

> Am I so dependent on body and senses that I cannot exist without these? But I was persuaded that there was nothing in all the world, that there was no heaven, no earth, that there were no minds, nor any bodies: was I not likewise persuaded that I did not exist? Not at all; of a surety I myself did exist since I persuaded myself of something [or merely because I thought of something]. But there is some deceiver or other, very powerful and very cunning, who even employs his ingenuity in deceiving me. *Then without doubt I exist also if he deceives me, and let him deceive me as much as he will, he can never cause me to be nothing so long as I think that I am something.* So that after having reflected well and carefully examined all things, we must come to the definite conclusion that this proposition: I am, I exist, is necessarily true each time that I pronounce it, or that I mentally conceive it. (HR I, 150; AT vii, 25; my emphasis)

Thus even if I am nothing but a thought in the mind of the demon deceiver, I am something. And a necessary truth is revealed, albeit a very sparse truth, but nevertheless a truth which is impervious to the power of the deceiver. Early on in the third *Meditation*, he writes:

> I am certain that I am a thing which thinks; but do I not then likewise know what is requisite to render me certain of a truth? Certainly in this first knowledge there is nothing that assures me of its truth, excepting the clear and distinct perception of that which I state, which would not indeed suffice to assure me that what I say is true, if it could ever happen that a thing which I conceived so clearly and distinctly could be false; and accordingly, it seems to me that already I can establish as a general rule that all things which I perceive very clearly and very distinctly are true. (HR I, 158; AT vii, 35)

Here we seem to close the "loop": a single truth *and* a matching criterion (clarity and distinctness) of its truth – the truth and the criterion are thus given *together*. Descartes clearly understood the Pyrrhonian dialectic. The truth and the criterion could not be separated, otherwise an opening would be created for the demon deceiver. For example, any appeal to the principles of logic would create openings for it! There could be several possible challenges: one would have to know that the principles of logic employed are true, one would have to know they have been applied to the premisses correctly, and if a conclusion were drawn, one would need to know that it had been drawn correctly. That is why the true proposition (*cogito* ...) and the criterion of truth (clarity and distinctness) had to come together and at once if the demon's power was to be deflected. But hold the possible challenges from the demon aside, why does Descartes think he can automatically, as it were, extend the "clarity and distinctness" criterion beyond the *cogito* experience? The demon deceiver is defeated only in this one instance. There is a great deal of work to do. The demon has yet to be exorcized. Until then, appeals to clarity and distinctness outside the *cogito* would seem to have no force.

Talk about demons may seem out of place in a philosophical discussion, but a few words on a trial that interested all Europe in the 1630s is in order. There was a very famous and much discussed witch trial[16] in Loudon which resulted in the condemnation of a local pastor, Fr. Urbain Grandier. The Ursuline nuns in a local convent were found to be possessed by devils. Over a period of several years, extended and intensive exorcisms were carried out. Viewing the exorcisms in all their virtually pornographic richness became a popular form of theater. Thousands of visitors came from all over Europe. In the end, the exorcisms were stopped, and the ultimate question was put to the possessed Prioress: who has bewitched you? Answer: Grandier. He was accused, tortured, tried, convicted, and in 1634, although never "confessing" his guilt, burned alive.

The trial raised the question of the status of demonic evidence and it is this which is philosophically interesting. After all, if a witch could bewitch judge and jury, how could truthful testimony be elicited? The failure to find a satisfactory way to handle those who were judged "possessed" is what gave rise to the notion of an *ordeal*. Ordeals are Catch-22 situations: if tied up, weighted down, and thrown into a pond, a real witch would not drown. The innocents drowned! We have continued to call certain political trials *witch trials* because, although formal exorcisms may partially be out of favor, there seems to be no way for an accused to prove his or her innocence. For example, if, in the course of a trial of someone accused of being a Communist in America in the 1950s, the accused brought distinguished and honorable people to speak in his or her defense, the rejoinder was elegant: the accused was guilty because only a Communist would be able to turn up such good character witnesses! Descartes does not mention Loudon, but witches and demons populated the landscape of Europe (and America) in the seventeenth and eighteenth centuries and even the Sorbonne had been obliged to rule on the status of demonic evidence. This is what the Sorbonne ruled:

> We the undersigned Doctors of the Faculty of Paris, touching certain questions which have been proposed to us, are of the opinion that one must never admit the accusation of demons, still less must one exploit exorcisms for the purpose of discovering a man's faults or for determining if he is a magician; and we are further of the opinion that, even if the said exorcisms should have been applied in the

presence of the Holy Sacrament, with the devil forced to swear an oath (which is a ceremony of which we do not at all approve), one must not for all that give any credit to his words, the devil being always a liar and the Father of Lies.[17]

It was also said that "the devil must not be believed, even when he tells the truth." So Descartes's idea of postulating a demonic deceiver would have resonated within the seventeenth-century world. Moreover, there were theological considerations. In his Objections to the *Meditations*, Mersenne challenges Descartes's claim that God neither lies nor is a deceiver. Indeed, Mersenne cites two scholastics who subscribe to the thesis that on occasion God has lied. Descartes denies that interpretation of the relevant biblical texts and hence sees no problem, but grants that *we* may sometimes be in error.

Descartes next seeks to find out *what* he is. Answer: he is a being whose whole essence is thinking. In order to try to get clearer about this, Descartes, in the second *Meditation*, turns to a simple sensed object, a piece of beeswax. It tastes sweet, it still has the odor of flowers, "its color, shape, and size are apparent." It is hard and cold, etc. "Thus everything which can make a body distinctly known are found in this example." But note what happens when we heat up the wax. Its taste evaporates, its color changes as it becomes clear, its shape changes radically, and its size increases. It can no longer be tapped as it is now in a liquid state. "Does the same wax remain after this change?" Yes. But this is not something perceived by the senses since *everything* we observed has changed.

> Let us attentively consider this, and, abstracting from all that does not belong to the wax, let us see what remains. Certainly nothing remains excepting a certain extended thing which is flexible and movable. But what is the meaning of flexible and movable? Is it not that I imagine that this piece of wax being round is capable of becoming square and of passing from a square to a triangular figure? No, certainly it is not that, since I imagine it admits of an infinitude of similar changes, and nevertheless do not know how to compass the infinitude by my imagination, and consequently this conception which I have of the wax is not brought about by the faculty of imagination. What now is this extension? Is it not also unknown? For it

becomes greater when the wax is melted, greater when it is boiled, and greater still when the heat increases; and I should not think that even this piece that we are considering is capable of receiving more variations in extension than I have ever imagined. We must then grant that I could not even understand through the imagination what this piece of wax is, and that it is my mind alone which perceives it. (HR I, 154–155; AT vii, 31)

This conception that he has of the wax is not achieved by the faculty of imagination but instead is conceived by the *pure understanding* without the benefit of any sensory contribution. Descartes's use of the piece of wax adds a bit of drama to his story, but in fact, any object would have done just as well. The pure understanding does not grasp the particular extension of the individual piece of wax. It grasps extension. Although I believe the interpretation is in error, it has often been tempting to read Descartes as if he were using a form of the primary/secondary quality distinction which John Locke (1632–1704) was to make famous in his *Essay Concerning Human Understanding* (1690).

Locke, who tends to subscribe to empiricism and who thus holds that our knowledge comes through the doors of our senses, maintains that material things have two sorts of qualities, primary and secondary: secondary or sensible qualities are not really in the object we perceive except insofar as those qualities can generate sensible ideas in us. A rose, for example, has an atomic structure of little particles which fall below the threshold of our senses. These particles interact with our own perceptual machinery (and nervous system) and generate the idea of the color of the rose. Strictly speaking, the rose is not colored. Nor are the atoms themselves. On the other hand, the solidity, extension, figure, motion, rest, and number (Locke's list varies) of the minute particles of the object constitute its *real* qualities and the ideas caused by these real or primary qualities generate ideas which map on to the real qualities of the object *and resemble them.*

Although it is often assumed that Descartes employs a pre-Lockian, so to speak, version of Locke's primary/secondary quality distinction, I have tried to make clear that Descartes grounds his knowledge of the piece of wax on very different principles. The extension apprehended by the pure understanding is not connected with any sensory object. As Descartes tells Mersenne in this connection, bodies themselves are not "perceived by sense, but they are perceived by the intellect alone" (HR II, 33; AT vii, 132). The point to the piece of wax exercise is to get us to appreciate that real knowledge of things resides not in anything having to do with the senses, but in the province of the intellect. We are enabled to understand that extension constitutes the essence of the material world, but that in grasping this essence we grasp *the essence of all possible material objects*. We gain no knowledge of this particular piece of wax in its particularity. Thus far, Descartes has yet to exorcise the demon, so the role he here ascribes to the pure understanding remains provisional – but that is the direction in which he is moving. As will be clear by the time he completes his *Meditations*, the wax's extension only alerts us to the essence of material things, and the basis for our *knowledge* of extension rests on innate ideas, not on anything sensed! At this point he only hints at his ultimate intentions, and falls back on saying that regardless of how weak our knowledge of material things may be, at every step we at least understand better the nature of the mind. Thus Descartes does not introduce anything like Locke's primary/secondary quality distinction. Writing in an early work, *The World* (1629–33 but not published until after his death), he writes in direct opposition to the view that a relation of resemblance holds between sensory data and things:

> Words, as you well know, bear no resemblance to the things they signify, and yet they make us think of these things, frequently even without our paying attention to the sound or the words or to their syllables. Thus it may happen that we hear an utterance whose meaning we understand perfectly well, but afterwards we cannot say in what language it was spoken. Now if words, which signify nothing except by human convention, suffice to make us think of things to which they bear no resemblance, then why could nature not also have established some sign which would make us have the sensation of light, even if the sign contained nothing in itself which is similar to this sensation? (CSMK I, 81; AT xi, 4)

It may be recalled that Montaigne (following Sextus) rejected the claim that perceptions could be assumed to resemble "external objects." If one has never seen Socrates, one has no grounds for saying that a portrait accurately resembles him. The "resemblance" claims made by Locke fly in the face of Sextus and Montaigne's thesis that there seems to be no way to establish a resemblance relation between perceptions and "external" things. Descartes's failure to enshrine a resemblance relation in his discussion of ideas and extension at the end of the Second *Meditation* fully accords with Montaigne's own rejection of the relation.

"But among these ideas, some appear to me to be innate"

The headings of two of the six meditations make reference to God. The title of the third *Meditation* reads, *Of God: that he exists.* This time, instead of turning to things in the world like the piece of wax, Descartes turns to the content of his thoughts. His problem is to eliminate the possibility that God is a deceiver. So he begins with sorting out his ideas. And our difficulties seem to stem from the fact that we make judgments that our ideas, ideas which are as it were neutral with respect to reality, conform or are similar to "things outside of myself." Ideas, taken in themselves, seem to fall into three classes: (1) some seem to be "elicited from certain notions that are innate in me" (HR I, 161; AT vii, 39), (2) some seem to come from without (i.e. adventitious); and (3) the rest can be made by [caused by] myself.[18]

It may seem that most ideas fall into the second category. We may be so inclined by custom and then be convinced by the fact that these ideas seem independent of our wills. When we open our eyes we can not will away what we see. Nor is there any guarantee that reality corresponds with our ideas. We seem to have one idea of the sun from our senses and another from astronomical considera- tion – the mathematical components of which "come from certain innate ideas" (35). There is a huge literature on what Descartes could possibly have meant by innate ideas.

The renewed interest in innate ideas was generated by Noam Chomsky's work in linguistics. But here are a few lines from Descartes's *Notes Directed against a Certain Programme*. It was directed against his one-time friend and erstwhile student Henricus Regius (1598–1679) at Utrecht.[19] The text was printed, in 1648, apparently without Descartes's knowledge:

> I never wrote or concluded that the mind required innate ideas which were in some sort different from its faculty of thinking; but when I observed the existence in me of certain thoughts which proceeded not from extraneous objects nor from the determination of my will, but solely from the faculty of thinking which is within me, then, that I might distinguish the ideas or notions (which are the forms of these thoughts) from other thoughts *adventitious* or *factitious*, I termed the former "*innate.*" (HR I, 442; AT viii b, 357–358)

He goes on to say:

> It follows that the ideas of the movements and figures are themselves innate in us. So much the more must the ideas of pain, colour, sound and the like be innate, that our mind may, on occasion of certain corporeal movements, envisage these ideas, for they have no likeness to the corporeal movements ... I should like *our friend* to instruct me as to what corporeal movement it is which can form in my mind any common notion, e.g. the notion that "*things which are equal to the same thing are equal to one another.*" (HR I, 443; AT viii b, 359–360)

Descartes's discussion of three sorts of ideas has not done the work that must be done. The demon deceiver has not yet been exorcized. Now he turns to considering ideas in terms of what they appear to represent, what they seem to be about.

The principle which Descartes chooses to drive his proof for the existence of God is that there must be as much reality "in the total efficient cause as in its effect. For, pray, whence can the effect derive its reality, if not from its cause?" (HR I, 162; AT vii, 40). Crudely, one can say that it takes a source of heat for an object to become hot. Alas, at this point Descartes's argument takes a number of very technical turns involving a variety of complex scholastic terms. But it seems to come down to this: if I check each of my ideas and search to see whether I possess sufficient reality to be the cause of these ideas, I come to appreciate that I might be the cause of almost all the ideas which I may encounter. Thus ideas which represent various objects to me might be the products of my imagination and fantasy. This holds, at least provisionally, for my "clear and distinct" ideas of material things and even for extension, the essence of the material world.

> But as to all the other qualities of which the ideas of corporeal things are composed, to wit, extension, figure, situation and motion, it is true that they are not formally in me, since I am only something that thinks; but because they are merely certain modes of substance (and so to speak the vestments under which corporeal substance appears to us) and because I myself am also a substance, *it would seem that they might be contained in me eminently.* (HR I, 165; AT vii, 44–45; my emphasis)

One might have thought that the radical distinction between mind and body, between thought and extension, was absolute. And yet here Descartes says that even extension could be contained in me eminently. This is surely a dangerous move because it jeopardizes the mind–body distinction in a way which threatens to encourage the mentalistic reading, the reading which sees all ideas of whatever ilk as being all there is in Descartes's framework. I don't think that is the way to understand Descartes, if only because a mentalistic reading can be given to any theory of knowledge – in the sense that any apparent instance of a non-mental counter-example can also be said to be mental, i.e. an "idea," since by the very perception or even thought of the non-mental item we can be said to have an "idea" of it "automatically," so to speak. And that proves more than most critics want to prove. "Eminently," on the other hand, is a term of art within scholastic thought and it means something like "in a superior fashion." That is, the various ideas are not to be understood as being on a par one with another.

Nevertheless, there is one idea with very special status: the idea of God is something which could not have come from me, since God is an infinite, eternal, immutable, independent, omniscient, and omnipotent substance – and I most certainly am not. The idea of *substance* "exists in me from the very fact that I am a substance." The idea of a perfect being I derive from the fact that I am an imperfect substance. And I know that I am *imperfect* because I am a doubting being. So the idea of God is not one which I could have generated from within myself. If I had that potential I would have given myself infinitely superior attributes! I come equipped with the idea of God. But by means of the causal principle cited above, Descartes believes he can move from the *idea* of a perfect substance (God) to the *existence* of that substance.

On occasion Descartes talks as if *I doubt, therefore I am* is a substitution instance of *I think, therefore I am* and that in one sudden, all-encompassing intuition of thought one is given (1) the solution to the criterion problem – thanks to the roles of clarity and distinctness, (2) perfection (essential for characterizing God) as the counterpart of our imperfection as revealed in our doubting, (3) thought as the essence of mind, (4) the notion of substance, i.e. the substantial self as the bearer of qualities, in this case mental qualities. Perhaps in this way Descartes intends to avoid claiming that each step is a step in an argument, because if the steps must be logically certified, then they are subject to the destructive force of the demon. Descartes appears to be taking (1) through (4) as constituents in one single axiom, so to speak, *an axiom which is apprehended in a single all-encompassing grasp.* Only in some such way does it seem possible for Descartes to achieve the goal he seeks. In any case, he believes that he has established a path from our nature to the *idea* of God and from that idea, by means of the causal principle, to the *existence* of God.

In the fourth *Meditation*, as part of his explanation of how error comes about, Descartes says that we have two faculties, the faculty of knowing, of conceiving, and the faculty of choice. Our faculty of conceiving is, however, greatly limited while our faculty of choice, the will, is apparently infinite. We have, Descartes believes, totally free wills. Error enters into the human condition because we often judge as true something which is doubtful. It is because we have trouble restraining the infinite will to matters which the intellect finds clear and distinct. How do we avoid error? We judge as true those things which we see with clarity and distinctness or at least as close to those criteria as we can get. We have a means for estimating the validity of evidence and we know we should not make precipitous judgments.

We do not, however, possess a faculty which stands as the source of error. Error arises because of (avoidable) mistakes we choose to make. As for our free will, Descartes simply asserts that our wills are totally free and that this is an absolute given in our experience. To repeat, it is asserted, it is not argued for. And Descartes never wavers in his commitment to this principle.

Given that from the beginning of recorded philosophic history the free will question has always been on the agenda, Descartes's approach may appear surprising. Are our actions "determined"? Are we programmed either "internally" or by our environment? Descartes does not discuss such matters. Our wills are free and that is the end of the story. Descartes writes to Gassendi in his Reply to the Fifth set of Objections:

> You next deny certain truths about the indeterminateness of the will; and although they are in themselves quite evident, I refuse to prove them before your eyes. For these matters are such that anyone ought to experience them in himself, rather than be convinced of them by ratiocination … Refuse then to be free, if freedom does not please you; I at least shall rejoice in my liberty, since I experience it in myself, and you have assailed it not with proof but with bare negations merely. (HR II, 224–225; AT vii, 377–378)

The fifth *Meditation* is entitled: "Of the Essence of Material Things and, once more, of God: that he Exists." Much of the heavy work in Cartesianism is laid out in this *Meditation*. Picking up from some ideas from the second *Meditation*, Descartes again speaks of an infinity of ideas in my thought (not my imagination). And these ideas, for example the properties of geometrical figures are eternal and immutable, and in no way depend on my mind, whereas the ideas of sense reflected in my imagination do. When I make complex mathematical discoveries, the ideas I encounter in my mind are not of my own mind's making. They are part of a store-house of innate ideas with which every human comes equipped. But whatever truths about material things I may demonstrate, whatever truths I apprehend as clear and distinct, bear only on the *essence* of those material things. There are no demonstrations that these essences map on to *existent* material things. More generally, as the titles of the *Meditations* show, we can say that Descartes is drawing a very sharp distinction between the essence and the existence of things. The essence of the material world, extension, is the subject-matter of geometry. It is not "in" the world of sense anymore than points, lines, and planes are.

Pencil lines on paper and chalk marks on blackboards may be useful for alerting us to think about points and lines, but skill in solving problems in geometry is not a matter of having sharp pencils. The stuff of mathematics is not sensed – for Descartes it is grasped by the pure understanding. He believes he has drawn a sharp, indeed an absolute distinction, between the world of concepts and the world of sensations and sensory ideas. Concepts are what they are, independent of our thinking of them, whereas sensations are mind-dependent. Yet he often speaks of all of them as "ideas" and that has made some critics say that everything is "mental" within the Cartesian system, despite Descartes's best efforts to make his distinction hard and fast. Or perhaps part of the difficulty arises from the fact that in his earliest (and unpublished in his lifetime) writings he allowed "imagination" to include "conception."

Having drawn a sharp distinction between essence and existence in the *Meditations*, a distinction that he believes holds for all things, he turns to God. "I clearly see that existence can no more be separated from the essence of God than can its having three angles equal to two right angles be separated from the essence of a [rectilinear] triangle." He adds: "so there is not any less repugnance to our conceiving a God (that is a Being supremely perfect) to whom existence is lacking (that is to say, to whom a certain perfection is lacking), than to conceive of a mountain which has no valley" (HR I, 181; AT vii, 66). This is known as the Ontological Argument and in various forms and guises it already appears in the medieval period. Descartes immediately takes up the standard refutation:

Still from the fact that I conceive of a mountain without a valley, it does not follow that there is such a mountain in the world; similarly although I conceive of God as possessing existence, it would seem that it does not follow that there is a God which exists; for my thought does not impose any necessity upon things, and just as I may imagine a winged horse, although no horse with wings exists, so I

could perhaps attribute existence to God, although no God existed.
(HR I, 181; AT vii, 67)

This, says Descartes, is sophistry. I cannot think of God *except* as existing. It is true that for chairs, tables, and mountains we can readily separate their existence from their essence. But God is a special case. He is not just a chair or table whose existence can be separated from his essence. God is a unique and supremely perfect being – not the sort of being whose existence is only possible. To consider God's existence as a mere possibility is to ignore the fact that God is a necessary being. The Ontological Argument, and the standard claim against it that existence can not be derived by logical moves, are both fully developed by Anselm of Canterbury (1033–1109). Thomas Aquinas, much concerned to establish God's existence by argument, did not accept this (Anselm's) argument, although strangely enough he did hold that in God existence and essence coincide. There are hundreds, if not thousands, of "refutations" of the Ontological Argument either in Descartes's or Anselm's version – or both. It is perhaps tempting to "refute" because all the elements in it can be seen almost in a single conceptual grasp. But the defense is simplicity itself: to argue against the proof you must have the idea of God. If you say that your idea of God is of an *imperfect* being, then you don't have the idea of that supremely perfect being in whom essence and existence are inseparable. If you say you don't have any idea of God then you can't enter the argument. It is doubtful, or so it seems to me, whether arguments for God's existence play any religious role. I leave that for others to decide, but it is perhaps worth noting that proofs for God's existence do not seem to enter into most religious discourse, religious activity, prayers, or hymns.

The fifth *Meditation* concludes with what has proven to be something of a philosophical puzzle. We have been presented with (at least!) two proofs for the existence of God. Now God is invoked to guarantee that all our *clear and distinct* perceptions are true. The difficulty is obvious. The steps whereby we establish the existence of God are clear and distinct – but we have no assurance that our *clear and distinct* ideas are true. Several of the philosophers who wrote "Objections" to the *Meditations* at the behest of Mersenne found these steps wanting. Although he was not the only Objector on this score, Antoine Arnauld's formulation is the best known.

> The only remaining scruple I have is an uncertainty as to how a circular reasoning is to be avoided in saying: the only secure reason we have for believing that what we clearly and distinctly perceive is true, is the fact that God exists. But we can be sure that God exists, only because we clearly and evidently perceive that; therefore prior to being certain that God exists, we should be certain that whatever we clearly and evidently perceive is true. (HR II, 92; AT vii, 214)

In the Cartesian literature this criticism is known as *Arnauld's Circle*. It is formulated in terse form and one might expect that Descartes would feel obliged to take it seriously. It appears to be the sort of criticism which could be taken to unravel his entire philosophy. But he doesn't see it as a devastating criticism. He simply sends Arnauld back to his Reply to Mersenne's somewhat similar objection. First, Descartes takes up the question of whether one logically deduces existence from thought in establishing the truth of *I think, hence I am, or exist*. If the *cogito* is a logical deduction then one must first establish that the principles of logic are sound *and* that one has made a correct application of those logical principles to the premises. Instead, in an altogether remarkable passage, Descartes says that he does *not* deduce existence from thought "by a syllogism, but, *by a simple act of mental vision*" (HR II, 38; AT vii, 140; my emphasis).

In the few sentences with which he replies to Arnauld he writes:

> There [in the Reply to Mersenne] I distinguished those matters that in actual truth we clearly perceive from those we remember to have formerly perceived. For first, we are sure that God exists because we have attended to the proofs that established this fact; but afterwards it is enough for us to remember that we have perceived something clearly, in order to be sure that it is true; but this would not suffice, unless we knew that God existed and that he did not deceive us. (HR II, 115; AT vii, 140)

Descartes admittedly discusses the role of memory at the end of the Fifth *Meditation*, as when a geometrical proof is recalled, but it is not clear how this clarifies matters. Many commentators have maintained that Descartes evaded and avoided Arnauld's criticism. Others have believed that Arnauld misunderstood the subtle pattern of the development of Descartes's argument. There are literally hundreds of essays on the question. But the Circle argument reminds one of the *Objection of Objections* which Gassendi posed. Gassendi, a priest and very able philosopher, was always a thorn in Descartes's side. Not only are his Objections to the *Meditations* the longest, but when he received Descartes's Replies to his Objections, he prepared Counter-Objections! With brevity and obvious irritation, Descartes responded to these in a letter to Claude Clerselier (1614–84) (usually included as a preface to Gassendi's Fifth set of Objections). One objection, however, clearly upset Descartes.

> Many people of great acumen are said to believe that they clearly see that the mathematical extension, which I take as the basal principle of my physics, is nothing but my thought, and that it has and can have no subsistence outside of my mind, being merely an abstraction that I form from a physical body; that consequently the whole of my physics is but imaginary and fictitious, as is likewise all pure mathematics: and that the physical nature of the real things that God has created requires a matter that is real, solid, and not imaginary. Here we have the *objection of objections*, and the sum of the whole doctrine of these men of great acumen who are here brought into evidence. (HR II, 131; AT ixa, 212; my emphasis)

Gassendi asks how it is possible to get "outside" one's ideas to an external "reality." And if one cannot, then one is in effect trapped within a private reality. Arnauld's argument does not take that form. But in effect he too wants to know how one can get outside the circle of one's ideas. Arnauld hammers away on the point that when Descartes uses God to guarantee the truth of his clear and distinct ideas, the steps in his argument are not themselves guaranteed, that is, we have not yet proved that God is not a deceiver. For reasons such as these, several commentators, especially in the eighteenth century, thought of Descartes as advancing the philosophical position known as *idealism*, i.e. that "strictly speaking" nothing but our ideas exist. I do not think Descartes falls into that category because I think the domain of mathematics which he defends is for him the real world, a world whose entities are what they are *entirely* independent of our thinking of or about them, entities which are neither imaginary nor fictitious.

I think the key to Descartes's solution to the problem of Arnauld's Circle rests on his appeal to *cogito, ergo sum*. Descartes appreciated the genius of the Pyrrhonian position. He understood that in order to claim that a proposition is true, the proposition must be judged in accordance with a criterion. Yet the criterion of truth itself requires that one know that the criterion is true, i.e. one already needs to know what is true in order to specify the criterion, but one needs to know the criterion in order to recognize its truth. Thus here we have a proposition which is true and which is provided with the criterion all in a single step.

"I, first of all men, upset the doubts of the sceptics"

The genius of Descartes's own position is that by grasping the truth of *cogito ergo sum* in a "simple act of mental vision," there is no way to generate the circularity of the criterion argument. Clarity and distinctness *and* the true proposition come in a seamless unit. Descartes may never have had a sceptical thought in his life, but he understood how to challenge the methodology of Pyrrhonism at its very foundation. Replying to Bourdin (1595–1653), Descartes writes that by means of his own arguments, "*I, first of all men, upset the doubts of the sceptics*" (HR II, 336; AT vii, 550; my emphasis).

Gassendi also objected to the *cogito*. "You might have inferred ['I am, I exist, is true each and every time that you pronounce it, or that you mentally conceive it.'] from any other activity, since our natural light informs us that whatever acts also exists" (HR II, 137; AT vii, 259). Descartes replies:

> You have no right to make the inference: *I walk, hence I exist*, except in so far as our awareness of walking is a thought; it is of this alone that the inference holds good, not of the motion of the body, which sometimes does not exist, as in dreams, when nevertheless I appear to walk. Hence from the fact that I think that I walk I can very well infer the existence of the mind which so thinks, but not

that of the body which walks. (HR II, 207; AT vii, 352)

Returning to Mersenne, who was not only troubled by the syllogistic appearance of *cogito ergo sum*, he also questioned Descartes's claim that "we could know nothing with certainty unless we were first aware that God existed" (HR II, 38; AT vii, 140). Descartes explains to Mersenne that he does not deny that an atheist can:

> know clearly that the three angles of a triangle are equal to two right angles ... I merely affirm that, on the other hand, such knowledge on his part cannot constitute true science, because no knowledge that can be rendered doubtful should be called science. Since he is, as supposed, an Atheist, he cannot be sure that he is not deceived in the things that seem most evident to him, as has been sufficiently shown; and though perchance the doubt does not occur to him, nevertheless it may come up, if he examine the matter, or if another suggests it; he can never be safe from it unless he first recognizes the existence of a God. (HR II, 39; AT vii, 141)

The "solution" recommended for the atheist is for him or her to follow the course of the *Meditations* – from the massive doubts and sceptical challenges through to the *cogito* and then finally to God as the guarantor of clear and distinct ideas. Only in that fashion can one arrive at "true science."

Descartes wants to make it very clear to Mersenne that even people who claim to know a falsity with certainty are not to be taken seriously.

> What is it to us, though perchance some one feigns that that, of the truth of which we are so firmly persuaded, appears false to God or to an Angel, and hence is, absolutely speaking, false? What heed do we pay to that absolute falsity, when we by no means believe that it exists or even suspect its existence? *We have assumed a conviction so strong that nothing can remove it, and this persuasion is clearly the same as perfect certitude.* (HR II, 41; AT vii, 145; my emphasis).

Descartes believes he is on solid ground because, unlike the person in error, he has built his case on clear and distinct ideas, God not being a deceiver, etc. He seems to think that the difficulty arises because the person in error is still confused about the status of sensations and confuses them with clear and distinct ideas. Error can and does occur in sensation, "as when one who is jaundiced sees snow as yellow … If any certitude does exist, it remains that it must be found only in the clear perceptions of the intellect" (HR II, 42; AT vii, 142). Descartes rejects empiricism and the reliability of sense experience. His commitment to rationalism remains constant.

Parenthetically, one may note that the Reformers were faced with a similar problem. Calvin had to answer the question: which book is the Bible? Answer: the Bible differs from all other books in being a text especially illuminated by God. The true meaning, the certain meaning of a given biblical text is the product of a reading by a person who is also illuminated. Thus double-illumination is required. Of course a problem remains when someone claims to be absolutely persuaded. Descartes's language of inner persuasion in relation to certainty is reminiscent of Calvin's position.

Mersenne not only challenges the status of the *cogito* by arguing that it is really syllogistically sustained, i.e. by principles of logic which themselves need to be certified. He also suggests that people often (incorrectly) maintain as clear and distinct propositions which turn out to be false – even in mathematics. I have indicated why Descartes believed that he had evaded the sceptic's demand that even his *clear and distinct* criterion itself stands in need of a criterion. Descartes dismisses the objection but Bishop Pierre-Daniel Huet (1630–1721), writing later in the century, culls a variety of objections from (especially) Mersenne's and Gassendi's criticisms and presents many of his own. He is furious with Descartes's "method of doubt" because he sees no mechanism for blocking what seems to him to be its universal corrosive impact. Accordingly, he questions the task of the *cogito* in this context and he attacks the *cogito* itself by challenging the unitary seamless simplicity Descartes ascribes to it. He argues that since a transition of thought must move from *cogito* to *ergo sum*, from "I think" to "therefore I am," the sceptical devices Descartes has unleashed can easily deprive Descartes's foundational principle of its crucial role in his philosophy and thereby relegate *cogito ergo sum* to the status of an ordinary complex syllogistic argument form subject to those very sceptical devices, e.g., challenges to logical principles and their application. A defender of the Jesuits in most matters, he accords primacy to faith over reason. He finds Descartes to be an arrogant person, contemptuous of the scholastic and Christian traditions, ignorant of Aristotelian physics and biology, and finally a person who conceals his sources, indeed, one who is not above stealing the ideas of others. He begins a tradition of increasingly violent attacks on Descartes which culminates in the writings of Pope John Paul II (see ch. 9 below).

The sixth and last *Meditation* is entitled: "Of the Existence of Corporeal Things and of the Real Distinction Between the Mind and the Body." We thus again have a contrast between the *essence* of material things and their *existence*, and once again Descartes places a conceptual barrier between the imagination and the power of conceiving, a power which resides in pure intellection. In imagination, the mind "turns toward the body." I can *conceive* of a chiliagon, a regular polygon of one thousand sides, but I cannot *imagine* the thousand sides of a chiliagon. My imagination is capable of imagining, say, a pentagon. But it is only in conception that I can calculate its area. In conception, I encounter an eternal essence, for example a triangle, which is reflected among our stock of innate ideas. Although our senses seem to tell us something about the material world, for a variety of reasons we cannot be sure our senses accurately report the nature of material things. Indeed, given the dream problem, there may be no real material world, although Descartes is inclined to rule that sceptical possibility out. But in the sixth *Meditation*, he takes up several sceptical moves not mentioned before. They are very traditional examples:

> Afterwards many experiences little by little destroyed all the faith which I had rested in my senses; for I from time to time observed that those towers which from afar appeared to me to be round, more closely observed seemed square, and that colossal statues raised on the summit of these towers, appeared as quite tiny statues when viewed from the bottom; and so in an infinitude of other cases I found error in judgments founded on the external senses. And not only in those founded on the external senses, but even in those founded on the internal as well; for is there anything more intimate

or more internal than pain? And yet I have learned from some persons whose arms or legs have been cut off, that they sometimes seemed to feel pain in the part which had been amputated, which made me think that I could not be quite certain that it was a certain member which pained me, even although I felt pain in it. (HR I, 189; AT vii, 76–77)

In spite of all his sceptical doubts, Descartes nevertheless says: "I do not think that I should doubt all of them universally." (HR 1, 190; AT vii, 78). Why not? "Because I know that all things which I apprehend clearly and distinctly can be created by God as I apprehend them." We can hold aside potential problems of interpretation over clarity and distinctness and puzzles over the status of the demon. But the fact is that we are not entitled to count sensory reports as knowledge because we *know* that they are never recorded with clarity and distinctness, and Descartes, despite the occasional rhetorical flourish, never alters his basic position on this matter.

Not surprisingly, in the seventeenth century there were already commentators who believed that if one seriously entertained the possibility of the demon deceiver, if one seriously entertained the possibility that the basic truths of mathematics could be rendered dubious by the demon, there could be no solution and no successful exorcism because there is then no longer a secure foundation for countering the demon. Others took a less stringent position: sensations never meet the requirement that they be perceived with clarity and distinctness and hence there is simply no basis for Descartes's claim to have closed the loop of doubt, so to speak, with the conclusion of the sixth *Meditation*. There is no way to solve the dream problem within Descartes's own terms. Instead, Descartes provides us with a totally secure domain of knowledge, knowledge which extends, for all practical matters, no further than mathematics. This may appear to limit sharply the domain of knowledge, but on the other hand, a level of claims which are only probable hardly qualifies as a level of knowledge. As far back as Plato, sensation did not qualify as a form of knowledge because while it may be infallible, that is, our sensory judgments are not subject to correction, sensation fails the second test for knowledge: sensory objects, existing only in the domain of flux, lack the independence (from the perceiver) required for objects of knowledge. For Descartes, there is one level of knowledge and that is the domain of the essence of the material world, and our knowledge of it is grounded in our innate ideas. If it is a material, i.e. an extended, thing, its essence is totally comprehended by geometry and arithmetic. Putting it dramatically, one might say that in knowing geometry and arithmetic one knows *all possible material objects*. What one does not know is whether any material object *exists*.

The "solution" Descartes provides for the dream problem appears in a single paragraph at the end of the *Meditations*:

> But when I perceive things as to which I know distinctly both the place from which they proceed, and that in which they are, and the time at which they appeared to me; and when, without any interruption, I can connect the perceptions which I have of them, with the whole course of my life, I am perfectly assured that these perceptions occur while I am waking and not during sleep. And I ought in no wise to doubt the truth of such matters, if, after having called up all my senses, my memory, and my understanding, to examine them, nothing is brought to evidence by any one of them which is repugnant to what is set forth by the others. For because God is in no wise a deceiver, it follows that I am not deceived in this. (HR I, 199; AT vii, 89)

Does our experience "cohere" in ways that allow us to avoid the force of the dream problem? Some followers of Descartes like Nicolas Malebranche thought that Descartes missed the destructive force of the argument he had himself formulated in the first *Meditation*. And so they restricted, as Descartes himself generally does, the domain of knowledge to what was clear and distinct. They thus did not count sense experience as a source of knowledge. Since Descartes does not, in this paragraph, claim that waking sense perceptions can ever be clear and distinct, perhaps he is not making a knowledge claim here. He may only be saying that we can distinguish waking from dream experiences but without the certainty needed for knowledge. That is hardly a very exciting way to end his *Meditations*!

Related to the question of whether Descartes, at the conclusion of the *Meditations*, finally resolves the dream and demon deceiver problems, is a judgment about the total force of the *Meditations*. Is Descartes a radical deductivist? Does he attempt to establish a deductive pattern whereby one moves by rigorous logical steps from the certainty of the *cogito* to the final dismissal of the dream and demon problems? Does he then move to "deduce" all of science, as some philosophers seem to have believed? I call that the "super-deductivist" reading of Descartes. It strikes me as aiming to provide a *reductio ad absurdum*, that is to force upon Descartes the absurd claim that by logically certified steps one can move from the logical certainty of the *cogito* to God and then to every detail in the world. This reading ignores the fact that Descartes did not subscribe to the ideology of empiricism but he was too good a scientist in too many fields not to recognize that he could not deduce the observed empirical data from any general principles. It does not seem to be the path Descartes follows if only because sensory as well as existential judgments are, for him, never grasped with clarity and distinctness. This is clear from the last paragraph (outlining the Sixth *Meditation*) in the Synopsis:

> Finally in the Sixth I distinguish the action of the understanding from that of the imagination; the marks by which this distinction is made are described. I here show that the mind of man is really distinct from the body, and at the same time that the two are so closely joined together that they form, so to speak, a single thing. All the errors which proceed from the senses are then surveyed, while the means of avoiding them are demonstrated, and finally all the reasons from which we may deduce the existence of material things are set forth. Not that I judge them to be very useful in establishing that which they prove, to wit, that there is in truth a world, that men possess bodies, and other such things which never have been doubted by anyone of sense; *but because in considering these closely we come to see that they are neither so strong nor so evident as those arguments which lead us to the knowledge of our mind and of God; so that these last must be the most certain and the most evident facts which can fall within the cognizance of the human mind.* (HR I, 142–143; AT vii, 15–16; my emphasis)

So we come to the very end of the *Meditations* and find that although the demon may have been exorcized, the extent of human knowledge in the strict sense is limited to the domain of essence. Descartes has thus followed through on his choice of titles for the fifth and sixth *Meditations* – titles in which essence and existence are sharply distinguished.

It is strange, but despite the role which it plays in his arguments, Descartes does not explain what "clear" and "distinct" mean in either the *Discourse* or the *Meditations*. He does this only in his *Principles of Philosophy* (Latin edition [*Principia Philosophiae*], 1644). The historical source for *clear and distinct* is not clear and distinct. Perhaps Descartes extracted it from a somewhat similar notion in Stoic philosophy or from Sextus's criticisms of the Stoic notion, or even from William of Ockham's uses of Duns Scotus's doctrine of intuitive cognition. In any event, here is Descartes's definition:

> I term that clear which is present and apparent to an attentive mind … [for example] as when we assert that we see objects clearly when, being present to the regarding eye they operate upon it with sufficient strength … But the distinct is that which is so precise and different from all other objects that it contains within itself nothing but what is clear. (*Principles*, I. xlv; HR I, 237; AT ixb, 22)

Thus clarity is a psychological standard. Something is clear when concepts are sharply presented. Distinctness, on the other hand, is a logical criterion. The idea of a triangle is distinct from that of a square because one can spell out in purely formal terms the geometrical elements which mark out the differences. In other words, clear and distinct seem to capture two very different things. Keeping this in mind is important as we reflect on the differences spelled out in the titles of the fifth and sixth *Meditations*, namely, the contrasts between essence and existence. If I am correct, the dream problem is never solved in the sixth *Meditation* because sensory judgments are never grasped with clarity and *distinctness* and so a "super-deductivist" interpretation cannot be sustained.

In the title of the sixth *Meditation* Descartes again speaks of the "real distinction between the mind and the body," and he repeats the point in the Synopsis of the *Meditations*:

> We cannot conceive of body excepting as indivisible, while the mind
> cannot be conceived excepting as indivisible. For we are not able to
> conceive of the half of a mind as we can do of the smallest of all
> bodies; so that we see that not only are their natures different but
> even in some respects contrary to one another. (HR I, 141; AT vii, 13)

A Synopsis is normally written after one has completed a piece of
writing, but that is not a disadvantage for the reader.

> In the first Meditation I set forth the reasons for which we may,
> generally speaking, doubt about all things and especially about mate-
> rial things, at least so long as we have no other foundations for the
> sciences than those which we have hitherto possessed. But although
> the utility of a Doubt which is so general does not at first appear, it is
> at the same time very great, inasmuch as it delivers us from every
> kind of prejudice, and sets out for us a very simple way by which the
> mind may detach itself from the senses; and finally it makes it impos-
> sible for us ever to doubt those things which we have once discovered
> to be true. (HR I, 140; AT vii, 12)

After turning to the soul and the importance of the real distinction
between soul and body, he turns his attention to various topics
which seem to get short shrift in the body of the *Meditations*.
Writing a Synopsis seems to concentrate an author's mind and I
think at this point Descartes presents a clearer account of what he
means by *substance* and his proof of *immortality* than he gives in the
body of his text.

> What I have said is sufficient to show clearly enough that the extinc-
> tion of the mind does not follow from the corruption of the body,
> and also to give men the hope of another life after death, as also
> because the premises from which the immortality of the soul may
> be deduced depend on an elucidation of a complete system of
> Physics. This would mean to establish in the first place that all
> substances generally – that is to say all things which cannot exist
> without being created by God – are in their nature incorruptible, and
> that they can never cease to exist unless God, in denying them his

concurrence, reduce them to nought; and secondly that body, regarded generally, is a substance, which is the reason why it also cannot perish, but that the human body, inasmuch as it differs from other bodies, is composed only of a certain configuration of members and of other similar accidents, while the human mind is not similarly composed of any accidents, but is a pure substance. For although all the accidents of mind be changed, although, for instance, it think certain things, will others, perceive others, etc., despite all this it does not emerge from these changes another mind: the human body on the other hand becomes a different thing from the sole fact that the figure or form of any of its portions is found to be changed. From this it follows that the human body may indeed easily enough perish, but the mind [or soul of man (I make no distinction between them)] is owing to its nature immortal. (HR I, 141; AT vii, 13–14)

Descartes's opponents, the atomists, hold that all things, and there are only material things, are composed of atoms and the void. Material objects cast off vast numbers of gossamer-like films in all directions. They are said to move at the speed of thought! Human perceivers are themselves constituted of atoms. Our sensory system is activated by the films. Films, in turn, pile up or "stack" in accordance with their similarity to one another, thereby generating materially based concepts by an overlay process, concepts which are thus directly derived from the material objects in the world. In this entirely empiricist way, all concepts may be said to be abstracted from things. And of course all such concepts retain a built-in relation of resemblance to the things from which they are abstracted.

Descartes takes matter's divisibility seriously because it fits with his attack on atomism. Generally, in the seventeenth century "atoms" were understood on the model of the ancient Greek philosophers, a model which had no scientific basis but which constituted a materialist story about "reality". Atoms, understood to possess as small a set of properties as a particular philosopher might specify (usually three or four, e.g. shape, motion, size and weight), lie behind the world of sense. Atoms are (virtually by definition) said to lie beneath the threshold of our senses. The materialist option, at least in the hands of the Greeks, was meant to characterize reality, i.e. the world and our place in it, in such a way that there was no "risk" of our having a soul or of being immortal. The materialists felt that priestly classes preyed (not prayed!) upon human anxiety about immortality and conned us into transferring our worldly goods to them. Thus a major reason for reducing reality to nothing but "atoms and the void" was to eliminate (separable) souls and thus to eliminate any entity which might be a candidate for immortality. Materialism has never been popular among religious groups, but on the other hand, the Divine Being could presumably always accord immortality to an especially nice cluster of shiny "mind" atoms – as most materialists always knew.

Here is Descartes, in a letter to Mersenne (30 September 1640) on the atom:

> First of all, an atom can never be conceived distinctly, since the very meaning of the word involves a contradiction, that of being a body and being indivisible. And as for a genuine part of matter, the determinate quantity of the space which it occupies is necessarily involved in any distinct thought which one can have of it. The principle aim of my metaphysics is to show which are the things that can be distinctly conceived. (CSMK III, 154; AT iii, 191–192)

Any line, or any three-dimensional object, can always be further divided. One has to admit that Descartes's treatment of matter is puzzling. Since extension constitutes the essence of matter, there is no such thing as empty space. It follows that a vacuum is an absurdity. His friend and mentor Beeckman held to both atoms and the void. However, he understood that atoms were solid entities. They had no elasticity. Hence Beeckman moved to a corpuscular position where bundles of atoms could be surrounded by the void – and there would then be space in which the atoms might move, squishy space, so to speak. Descartes favored a highly complex arrangement of vortices all under the creative power of God as befits a philosopher who assigns all *real* causal agency to God. The theory is spelled out in the *World* and also in his *Principles of Philosophy*.

As noted at the outset, empiricists hold that our knowledge arises from our sense experience. Rationalists reject that position and hold that the roots of human knowledge lie in our minds. The first philosopher to subscribe to rationalism is usually said to have been Plato and, roughly speaking, one may think of Descartes's domain of concepts as a Platonic domain, populated by entities not derived from sense experience. The empiricist tradition, on the other hand, usually subscribes to some form of abstractionism in order to account for how the mind forms concepts of things. Already among the pre-Socratics (Socrates: 469–399 BC) the atomists, as noted, developed an abstractionist model of concept formation, one which was further enriched by Democritus (460–357 BC) and Epicurus (341–271 BC).

When Mersenne arranged for the seven sets of objections to the *Meditations*, two of the authors were inclined toward materialism. Thomas Hobbes, the English philosopher, subscribed to a largely materialist position. Pierre Gassendi actually writes his objections to the *Meditations* from a materialist standpoint. He makes fun of Descartes by addressing him: *O Mind*. Descartes responds: *O Flesh*. More straightforward materialist objections to Descartes appeared from the eighteenth century onwards.

Neither Aristotle nor his medieval followers were attracted to atomism, but they usually remained abstractionists. They were not materialists but they were generally sympathetic to Aristotle's "proof" that all our knowledge was rooted in, and abstracted from, our sense experience. From Aristotle to Locke (cf. *Essay* II, iv, § 5 & 6) philosophers within the empiricist tradition held that the empiricist basis for our knowledge could be established with an elegant proof: a person lacking a sense channel could not know the quality appropriate to the missing channel. The blind man, for example, could not know color.[20] Hence all our knowledge came from our sense experience. It is perhaps clearest in Aquinas because he answers the question: "Does the soul understand all things through innate ideas?"

> The falseness of this opinion [Plato's innateness thesis] is clearly proved from the fact that if a sense be wanting, the knowledge of what is apprehended through that sense is also wanting. Thus, a man who is born blind can have no awareness of colors. This would not be

the case if the soul had innate likenesses of all intelligible things. (*Summa Theologica* I, Q LXXXIV, art. 3 [transl. John F. Anderson])

The difficulty with the many proofs which take this form is that the claim that the blind have no awareness of colors comes down to the trivial truth that blind people can't see. Presumably, when one asserts that a person born blind can have no awareness of color one is making some sort of scientific, i.e. empirical claim about blind people, and hence it ought to amount to something more than a supposed truth. What is more is it true that blind people can have no awareness of color? They can't see the stop light but they know perfectly well what color stop lights have. Blind people can also write and there seems to be no way to tell from their writings that they are blind – unless they tell us. All of which is to say that this particular sort of proof of abstractionism as a method of concept formation is not very convincing.

As briefly noted above, Aristotle holds that all things are composites of form and matter. In a thumb-nail sketch it is unfortunately easier to say what form and matter are not, rather than what they are. "Form" is not shape, it is not an image; it is closer in meaning to "formula." The form (or "formula") of a tree is its principle of growth and this serves as the basis for our knowledge of the tree. First, the form must be abstracted from the object. The form/matter composite can be pictured in our sensory apparatus but only then does the mind act on this form/matter composite represented in the sensory apparatus. The mind *immaterializes* the form from its material substrate and thereby provides the basis for the abstracted concept which is perhaps to be understood as reflected in word(s). Note that the unstructured immaterializing power of the mind does not introduce innate ideas. The objectivity and the content of our knowledge rests ultimately on data provided by the senses. Abstractionism is the defining characteristic of empiricism. It is how the mind gets "stuffed" – how our *blank tablets*[21] come to be written upon. Whether in its Aristotelian or its atomist versions, there is no room for innate ideas. On the other hand, on the Aristotelian model, because the abstracted forms (but not the matter), are *identical* to the forms in material things, the objectivity of our knowledge, i.e. the link of our mind to the world, is said to be preserved.

Descartes may have created problems for the atomists, but has Descartes provided us with a demonstration of the immortality of the soul in his own system? The term is used in the Synopsis but it is clear that what Descartes claims he has demonstrated is the real distinction between the mind and the body. In the latter part of the sixth *Meditation*, Descartes talks about the brain. He holds that the data of sense are transmitted (not always with total accuracy) to the brain, and the brain event precipitates a sensation in the mind. So although he maintains that the mind and the body are distinct substances, they are nevertheless intimately connected. In a letter to Huygens (1596–1687) [10 October 1642] Descartes writes:

> I think I know very clearly that [our souls] last longer than our bodies, and are destined by nature for pleasures and felicities much greater than those we enjoy in this world. Those who die pass to a sweeter and more tranquil life than ours; I cannot imagine otherwise. We shall go to find them some day, and we shall still remember the past; because we have, on my view, an intellectual memory which is independent of the body. (CSMK III, 216; AT iii, 598)

As noted above, immortality is also mentioned in the Dedication to the *Meditations* in the context of Descartes's explanation that he is pursuing Pope Leo X's injunction that Christian philosophers should refute the doctrines of those who hold that on grounds of natural reason (i.e. without the benefit of divine revelation) the individual soul perishes with the body. This is considered to be Averroes's interpretation of Aristotle. Given the Aristotelian form/matter distinction, the soul or mind is taken to be the form of the human being. But this form holds across the entire species and does not authorize *personal* immortality. For that reason Aquinas rejected the Averroistic reading of Aristotle (Christian Averroists were often obliged to rely directly on faith at this point) and was obliged to introduce several different principles of "individuation." In general, matter is what individuates things within their species for Aristotle. Dogs, for example, are all members of the same species. The same form is instantiated within each one. But what individuates one dog within the species, and hence from all the other dogs, is the matter which constitutes it. The matter of each dog is different, not the form.

Scholastics committed to the Aristotelian framework and wishing to avoid the Averroistic problem with respect to personal immortality had also to find a way to individuate angels. One answer was to say that there was angelic matter in angels! Aquinas solves the problem of individuating angels by counting *each* angel as a separate species (and hence not in need of further individuation). For religious reasons Aquinas obviously also wants to accord a special status to the human mind or soul. Otherwise one would not be able to talk sensibly of the immortality of the soul. He does not wish to make talk about immortality a matter of pure faith. Instead, he holds that although the mind or soul is the form of the human body, *it can have activities in which the body does not share.*[22] This is to consider the mind to be virtually an independent being, almost a substance – and no longer a mere form in accordance with traditional Aristotelian form/matter teaching. How then does each human mind, if it lacks a material component, get individuated? By an *act of existence* unique to it.

Descartes does not accept the Aristotelian framework and the form/matter distinction which stands at its center. But strangely enough there is room in his account for individual acts of existence which could conceivably provide a basis for individuating minds. That is because Descartes believes in continuous creation. Our being does not "coast" as it were, from one moment to another. Rather, it must be recreated, as he says in the third *Meditation*, at each successive instant: "the light of nature shows us clearly that the distinction between creation and conservation is solely a *distinction of reason*" (clearly stated in the Latin edition; my emphasis; HR 1, 168; AT vii, 49). In this way, God is the only true causal agent and God thus provides individuation for each human mind. Matter plays no part in this individuating process. As for a distinction of reason, this is scholastic terminology meaning a distinction drawn by the mind rather than a real distinction in things. With a real distinction, the distinguished elements or parts can, for example, be spatially separated.

Some philosophers have been uncomfortable about any immortality possibilities for Cartesian minds. P. F. Strawson (1919–), for example, worries that as memories rooted originally in our bodies fade, our disembodied survival becomes increasingly attenuated. "No doubt it is for this reason that the orthodox have wisely insisted on the resurrection of the body."[23] It is not clear how the resurrection of the body supports Strawson's opinion since if memories are truly rooted only in our bodies, embodied survival would also seem to run the risk of "attenuation." But recall what Descartes said: we have an *intellectual* memory which is independent of the body.

To the Most Serene Princess Elisabeth: "I consider this work [the *Principles*] ... due to you"

Princess Elisabeth (1618–80), daughter of Frederick, king of Bohemia and Elisabeth Stuart (daughter of James VI of Scotland and I of England), became interested in Descartes's philosophy and in 1643 he began a correspondence with her which continued until his death. It is a remarkable correspondence if only because it is one of the few times when Descartes expresses his feelings. Her philosophical query to him troubles all mind–body dualist philosophies: how can an immaterial soul act upon a material body – and vice versa?

In the *Discourse* and in his later writings Descartes presented an account of the sensations, an account which Elisabeth found unsatisfactory. Bodily activity is understood as mechanical. Sensory data is transmitted from the sense organs to the brain by means of tubes through which the animal spirits course. Although the soul, writes Descartes, "is joined to the whole body, there is yet in that a certain part in which it exercises its functions more particularly than in all the others."

> The part of the body in which the soul exercises its functions immediately is in nowise the heart, nor the whole of the brain, but merely the most inward of all its parts, to wit, a certain very small gland which is situated in the middle of its substance and so suspended above the duct whereby the

animal spirits in its anterior cavities have communication with this in the posterior, that the slightest movements which take place in it may alter very greatly the course of these spirits. (HR I, 345–346; AT xi, 352) [24]

The gland in question is the pineal gland. Descartes takes it to be centrally located deep in the brain and that it serves to unify, for example, the double impressions which come from the eyes. It is "the principal seat" of the soul. It is a bodily part where the interaction between the mind and the body takes place. It is where the corporeal interacts with the mental. It is where the mind imposes its will, or at least interacts, with the body. Descartes was a competent and knowledgeable physiologist for his time, but our understanding of mind–body interaction does not seem to be greatly enhanced by the discussion of the pineal gland! Princess Elisabeth forces him to admit that the relationship between mind and body is, in the end, inconceivable. But perhaps we should withhold judgment until we have thought about other "solutions" to the interaction problem.

Moving on from Princess Elisabeth and the interaction problem, there is another matter which bothered Descartes's contemporaries and which is a source of anti-Cartesian sentiment today. It is true that Descartes takes our bodies, and the bodies of animals, to be machines. He was, after all, a physicist and the science of matter was physics and his physics was mechanics. But he especially wants no blurring of distinctions which might incline us to think of matter as other than inert. Nevertheless in his Reply to the Sixth set of Objections [a set of questions from several theologians and philosophers, collected by Mersenne] to the *Meditations*, he writes:

As for dogs and apes, even though I were to grant that thought existed in them, it would in nowise follow that the human mind was not to be distinguished from the body, but on the contrary rather that in other animals also there was a mind distinct from their body.

He adds:

The people who affirm that dogs when awake know that they run [etc.] as if they could take up their station in the animals' hearts, really assert this merely and do not prove it. (HR II, 244; AT vii, 426)

After all, we have no direct access to any mind but our own, so it should come as no surprise that Descartes then says that we lack access to the "hearts" of animals. However, he is willing to assert that: "I have neither denied to the brutes what is vulgarly called life, nor a corporeal soul, nor organic sense" (HR II, 244; AT vii, 426). None of these admissions weakens his case for dualism, contrary to the hopes of his critics.

As Gaukroger (1950–) notes, Descartes stands by this position:

> For Descartes it is an empirical question whether animals have rational souls, and the cognitive and affective states that go with this. He tells Gassendi that whether we say an animal can think or not is something that can only be settled by *a posteriori* investigation of its behaviour; and to More he writes that "though I regard it as established that we cannot demonstrate that there is any thought in animals, I do not thereby think it is demonstrated that there is not, since the human mind does not reach into their hearts." Indeed, I am inclined to agree with the view that Descartes continually confines himself to the negative consideration that we cannot demonstrate the presence of rational souls in animals, that his main positive claim on this question is that the traditional justifications for attributing consciousness to animals are vacuous. (Gaukroger, 288–289)

The Princess may have forced Descartes's hand on the interaction question. It is clear that she has a keen mind and good philosophical sense and it is not obvious that she is persuaded by him. Still, Descartes dedicates his *Principles of Philosophy* (Latin, 1644) to her. His last philosophical work, *The Passions of the Soul* (French, 1649), was written largely in response to questions raised by the Princess and it too was dedicated to her. He emerges as her philosophical guide, her guru, her medical and psychological advisor. There are hints that he was in love with her, or at least he writes to her with some warmth:

> As I was passing through The Hague en route to France, it occurred to me that I ought to write and assure Your Highness that my ardour [Fr. *zéle*] and devotion will not alter even though I am changing my place of abode. (Letter to Princess, 6 June 1647; CSMK III, 323; AT v, 59)

However, Descartes tended to avoid personal encounters with her even when they lived not far apart.

The *Principles of Philosophy*, published as already noted in 1644, was translated (but not by Descartes) from his Latin. The French translation appeared in 1647. It is a long text, and is divided into four parts: (1) "The Principles of Human Knowledge," primarily Descartes's metaphysical doctrines; (2) "The Principles of Material Things," i.e. his physics; (3) "Of the Visible World," i.e. the application of his physics to the universe; (4) "The Earth." Each part is divided into short sections.[25] The text comes with a long letter to the translator, the Abbé Claude Picot (about 1601–68). Descartes says it may serve as a Preface to the French edition. It again afforded Descartes the opportunity to make some nasty remarks about Henricus Regius (1598–1679). This is followed by a letter (originally in Latin) dedicating the work to Princess Elisabeth.

Descartes's respect for and admiration of Princess Elisabeth must have been considerable. Otherwise he surely would not have dedicated the *Principles* (as well as the *Passions of the Soul*) to her. These are serious and difficult works. There is not a hint of condescension in his letter of dedication to her at the opening of the *Principles*. Descartes clearly believed that she would be able to understand them. And it should be kept in mind that she had no political influence, no wealth, indeed, no power. Worse, she was a Protestant!

As the heading for the first article of the *Principles*, First Part, reads, we are not far from the issues discussed in the *Meditations*. Indeed, in some respects, Descartes generally uses the *Principles* to spell out at length and in some detail issues already discussed in the *Meditations*, perhaps because he felt that the very brevity of the *Meditations* was a source of difficulty. Very few philosophers were as concerned with making their message as clear and straightforward as was Descartes. The struggle for clarity was not, as he quickly discovered, always greeted with cheerful acceptance. He begins: "That in order to examine into the truth, it is necessary once in one's life to doubt of all things, so far as this is possible" (HR I, 219; AT viiia, 5 ff). The heading of the second Principle reads: "That we ought to consider as false all those things of which we may doubt."

He then proceeds to discuss in terse style many of the topics discussed in the *Meditations*, for example, the dream problem as grounds for doubting the existence of sensible things, and the deceiver problem as a basis for doubting mathematical demonstrations. The *cogito* appears in article seven, and in eleven, "How we may know our mind better than our body," Descartes tightens up some topics he discussed earlier.

> But in order to understand how the knowledge which we possess of our mind not only precedes that which we have of our body, but is also more evident, it must be observed that it is very manifest by the natural light which is in our souls, that no qualities or properties pertain to nothing; and that where some are perceived there must necessarily be some thing or substance on which they depend ... We certainly observe many more qualities in our mind then in any other thing, inasmuch as there is nothing that excites us to knowledge of whatever kind, which does not even much more certainly compel us to a consciousness of our thought. To take an example, if I persuade myself that there is an earth because I touch or see it, by that very same fact, and by a yet stronger reason, I should be persuaded that my thought exists; because it may be that I think I touch the earth even though there is possibly no earth existing at all, but it is not possible that I who form this judgment and my mind which judges thus, should be non-existent; and so in other cases. (HR I, 223; AT viiia, 9–10)

Descartes thus insists that all qualities must inhere in a substance. And these various mental qualities must inhere in a mind because of their necessary link to consciousness, as the last sentence above holds. Thus even were it possible to give a mechanical (physical) account of the mental, every step would first be formed in our judgment and the existence of the material would always have to yield to the priority to be accorded the mental. In *Principle* twenty-one, Descartes devotes a few lines to "continuous creation," the doctrine (mentioned above) that at every moment we are totally dependent on God and that he must continuously re-create us.

> From the fact that we now are, it does not follow that we shall exist a moment afterwards, if some cause – the same that first produced us – does not continue to produce us; that is to say, to conserve us. And we

can easily recognise that there is no strength in us whereby we may conserve ourselves. (HR I, 227–228; AT viiia, 13)

In *Principles* forty-nine and fifty (Part 1), Descartes briefly mentions innate ideas, eternal truths. He says we can't give a list of them, but they include the so-called common notions or axioms, terminology which already appears in Euclid's *Elements* (the Greek source for geometry). If our minds are free of prejudices, at least some of these ideas may be apprehended with clarity and distinctness. But from the fact that these innate ideas, the basis for all mathematics, are in each mind, it does not follow that each person starts out knowing everything! Discoveries must be made even if their foundations are grounded in innate structures. Because we share common structures we can share common understanding.

Reminiscent of the Sixth *Meditation*, he writes (Part 1, Principle 60):

We can conclude that two substances are really distinct one from the other from the sole fact that we can conceive the one clearly and distinctly without the other. For in accordance with the knowledge which we have of God, we are certain that He can carry into effect all that of which we have a distinct idea. That is why from the fact that we now have, e.g. the idea of an extended or corporeal substance, although we do not yet know certainly whether such really exists at all, we may yet conclude that it may exist; and if it does exist, any one portion of which we can demarcate in our thought must be distinct from every other part of the same substance. Similarly because each of us is conscious that he thinks, and that in thinking he can shut himself off from himself all other substance, either thinking or extended, we may conclude that each of us, similarly regarded, is really distinct from every other thinking substance and from every corporeal substance. And even if we suppose that God had united a body to a soul so closely that it was impossible to bring them together more closely, and made a single thing out of the two, they would yet remain really distinct one from the other notwithstanding the union … those things which God can separate, or conceive in separation, are really distinct. (HR I, 243–244; AT viiia, 28–29)

As in the sixth *Meditation*, Descartes here separates our idea of corporeal substance from its existence. Unlike the mind, our knowledge of the existence of corporeal substance is restricted to its possible, and not its certain, existence. The radical distinction between mind and body remains one of those apparently insoluble puzzles. People seem to accept that there is a common-sense difference between consciousness on the one hand, and what we are conscious of on the other. Should this distinction provide a basis for construing minds and bodies as separate substances? Certainly in the last century, philosophers have tended to answer "no." And yet efforts to dissolve the distinction by reducing all matter to mind, or all mental things to matter, run into difficulties. Philosophers are uncomfortable with Cartesian-style dualism even when it seems to accord with our intuitions. Our thoughts and feelings do not seem to be equivalent to brain waves or electrical activity or chemical interactions.

When Descartes gave us a new account of human nature he turned the European intellectual world upside down. The acceptance of dualism, or even warring against dualism, meant that new ideas percolated through every corner of the so-called Republic of Letters. From hard science to "soft" science, from theology to philosophy, from politics to education, Descartes' fingerprints seem omnipresent. They are so omnipresent that we often no longer notice them, and then, in contradictory fashion, we often seem to be angry at his pervasive influence – as if we cannot escape his dominance except by the dubious route of denying it.

In the twenty years Descartes spent in The Netherlands, he came to know everyone who was anyone. He knew the philosophers and scientists associated with the universities in Utrecht, Leiden, and Groningen as well as in Franeker, and in the Illustrious Schools in Harderwijk and Deventer.[26] This widely dispersed circle of friends and acquaintances thus constituted a sounding box, so to speak, for Cartesian ideas. As has been noted, Descartes did not take kindly to criticism, and he doesn't seem to have been prepared for the waves of criticism which emerged first from Utrecht and then from Leiden. Often the critics had not read a word of Descartes – a phenomenon not unusual then or now in the Republic of Letters. Some years later Malebranche wryly commented that the least a critic should do is to read the book he is criticizing.

Descartes's Dutch critics were generally theologians. And their objections to Descartes's views often fall into patterns which one can also observe in the Objections to the *Meditations*. A frequent source of unease was that Descartes was understood to be rejecting Aristotelianism. And that was understood to mean that Descartes rejected the primacy of sense experience. Moreover, his method of doubt was taken to mean that he was himself a sceptic and that he was advocating scepticism and thus undermining religion and morality. Descartes was also often seen as rejecting the substantial union of soul and body and thereby threatening the intelligibility of the Christian doctrine of the resurrection of the body as well as the whole cluster of ideas surrounding essences, species, and genera – notions which had been embedded in Western thinking for more than a millennium. Descartes was also often condemned for being a papist. However, the occasional theologian noted wryly that those very same critics neglected to notice that they were themselves entirely indebted to scholastic (i.e. papist!) philosophy.

Innate ideas were also a source of complaint especially when steps to knowledge of God were taken to require innate ideas. And perhaps nothing so annoyed Descartes's critics as much as his "method of doubt." Those who bothered to read the *Meditations* were appalled to find the use of the demon deceiver. It was an easy next step, many critics felt, to atheism. That is, once scepticism was free to flourish, religious positions would be subjected to sceptical challenge, the authority of the theologians and the Synods would be undermined, and the way would be clear to establish atheism. From the late 1630s and for the next century, the Dutch intellectual community was enmeshed in controversy over Cartesianism. Sometimes the universities banned even the mention of Descartes's name, no less his ideas. But then they often turned the other way, perhaps because they hoped to keep the disputes under control. It is safe to say that through all the discussions and rows, Descartes was often badly advised on what to say, but more often than not, he refused to accept advice even when it promised to be useful. The net effect of these controversies was that Descartes became widely known and his ideas percolated through generations of practitioners of Dutch science and philosophy.

As already noted, the Protestant community, or at least the orthodox component of it, generally constructed their theology on an Aristotelian and scholastic base. Gerard de Vries (1648–1705) published a huge tome (in Latin) which became a standard textbook in the latter part of the seventeenth century in Protestant universities in Scotland and Ireland as well as in The Netherlands. Although Calvin himself defended innate ideas, De Vries was a fierce and intemperate critic of Descartes's appeal to innateness. Like many philosophers and theologians of the period, he feared that if one undermined the material base of our knowledge, if one denied that our knowledge was grounded in a material world which was apprehended in our sense experience, we would be deprived of those secure steps whereby we could prove the existence of God. This line of attack on Descartes had already been opened up in the Utrecht and Leiden debates.

The Dutch universities, and more generally Calvinism, provided a surprisingly fertile terrain for the early development of Cartesian ideas, as well as criticism of them. Following the Synod of Dordrecht (1618–19), an international congress which sought, without total success, to define Calvinist orthodoxy, Calvinism in The Netherlands was in continual ferment, with rigorous debates over the role of reason in matters of faith, salvation and justification, God's foreknowledge, free will, and the authority of clerical bodies to police religious ideas and practices within the Reformed communities. From 1640 on, Descartes's influence was paramount in Reformed circles in both The Netherlands and in France.

Two of the Objections to the *Meditations* generally receive less attention than those by more famous philosophers. The First is by Johan de Kater (Caterus) [d.1656], a priest in Alkmaar, a small city northeast of Amsterdam. De Kater's comments deal with Descartes's discussion of God, especially in the third and fifth *Meditations*. It is cast in genial and friendly terms on both sides. But the seventh set of objections, those by Pierre Bourdin, SJ (1595–1653), a fellow graduate of La Flèche, greatly distressed Descartes. We know that Descartes wanted the Jesuits to give a seal of approval to the *Meditations*. He may even have hoped that his work would be incorporated into Church teachings as Aquinas's had been centuries before. To his very good friend Constantijn Huygens (1596–1687) (father of the brilliant scientist Christiaan (1629–95), in whose education Descartes had been interested), Descartes wrote on 31 January 1642:

> Perhaps these scholastic wars will result in my *World* being brought into the world. It would be out already, I think, were it not that I want to teach it to speak Latin first. I shall call it Summa Philosophia to make it more welcome to the scholastics, who are now persecuting it and trying to smother it before its birth. The ministers are as hostile as the Jesuits. (CSMK III, 209–210; AT iii, 523)

At the very least Descartes hoped that the members of the Order from whose school he had graduated would not set about attacking him. However, that is precisely what happened. Bourdin was so harsh and condemnatory of Descartes that Descartes resorted to writing to his superior, Father Dinet. As noted, Descartes hoped to have the Jesuits put a blessing on his work. He was not sure, however, whether Bourdin was "his own person" or, as Descartes feared, whether he was really writing on behalf of the Jesuit order. Bourdin ran through a number of objections which troubled him, and which also bothered the Jesuits. Bourdin wrote at length against the method of doubt. The notion that one should cast aside all of one's prejudices, all the traditional ideas which one had, seemed like folly to Bourdin. The Church had always taken the role of "Tradition" seriously as a vehicle for defending the Faith against Protestants and other heretics. Bourdin feared, like the Calvinist critics, that Descartes's apparently indiscriminate use of scepticism would have as its consequence the erasing of *everything*. He also finds Descartes's comments on mind, soul, body, and substance philosophically muddled and generally unsatisfactory. Bourdin was not an incompetent philosopher, but that is how Descartes treated him. Descartes's Reply is so harsh that one wonders why he thought his next step was prudent, namely his appeal to the Provincial of the French Jesuits (Jacques Dinet – he had been one of Descartes's teachers at La Flèche) to complain about the treatment he had received at the hands of Bourdin. It is even an occasion for complaining yet again about the treatment he received both from

Gysbertus Voetius and from the (Calvinist) Utrecht authorities. The answer to why he wrote to Dinet appears in his letter to Mersenne of 30 September 1640. He writes: "I must confess that the quibbles of Father Bourdin have made me determine to fortify myself henceforth with the authority of others, as far as I can, since truth by itself is so little esteemed" (CSMK III, 153; AT iii, 184).

For the balance of the century, the Jesuits mounted a series of campaigns against Descartes. They most certainly had no intention of satisfying one of Descartes's dreams, namely of being (in effect) *the* Doctor of the Order. Rather they rejected his definition of substance, they refused to countenance extension as an essential attribute of substance, and they saw no way whereby Descartes could produce an account of transubstantiation within his system. The issue of scepticism came up repeatedly – as it did among the Calvinist theologians. Descartes might think that scepticism was a useful device for cleansing the mind of falsities so that the pursuit of knowledge might proceed unhindered, but his opponents seemed to think that once started, there was no stopping the Pyrrhonian dialectic. Belief in God, morality, religion, science, would all be swept up in the ensuing chaos. There were several condemnations of Descartes by Jesuits and finally in 1691 the University of Paris condemned him, although his writings had already been placed on Rome's *Index of Prohibited Books* (1663). Descartes's writings were placed on the *Index* "subject to correction" but they were uncorrected and they remained on the *Index*. A particularly sensitive issue was Descartes's denial of the existence of "real accidents." These were held to be essential to what many theologians counted as the "correct" formulation of the doctrine of transubstantiation. To Arnauld, who raised the question in the Fourth Objections to the *Meditations*, Descartes replied:

> As a matter of fact, never, to my knowledge at least, has the Church in any passage taught that the semblances [Lat. *species*] of the wine and bread that remain in the Sacrament of the Eucharist are real accidents of any sort which, when the substance in which they inhered is removed, miraculously subsist by themselves. (HR II, 119; AT vii, 252)

The Jesuits persisted in their attacks on Descartes, and later, on Malebranche. They were extremely severe on Yves-Marie André, himself a Jesuit (1675–1764). He was a follower of both Descartes and Malebranche (he was the author of a biography of Malebranche) and the Jesuits repeatedly condemned him and subjected him to the most rigorous inquisitions, but he refused to compromise his beliefs and was sentenced to a year in the Bastille. He lived long enough to see the Jesuits suppressed (1762). All of which suggests that the Jesuits were extremely committed to extirpating such traces of Cartesianism as they could find. It was altogether a most remarkable policy, not unlike similar efforts in our own days to try to cleanse society of ideas deemed dangerous.

"Grammar is to mind as geometry is to matter"

One reason Descartes is called the Father of Modern Philosophy is that he set the agenda for those philosophers (and theologians) who came after him. Whether they liked his views or not, whether they found his arguments compelling or whether they made every effort to refute them, the issues and their formulations were tainted by Cartesianism. Mersenne and those he enlisted to write the Objections to the *Meditations* were, whether pro or con, among the first Cartesians. Some, like Antoine Arnauld (1612–94), wove Cartesian ideas into what was often an anti-Cartesian position. He wrote volumes of criticism directed against Malebranche, but he also wrote two books which remained influential for two centuries. The historically more important one was his logic, *L'art de penser*. Co-authored with Pierre Nicole (1625–94), the book, popularly known as the *Port Royal Logic*, was published in 1662. Two years before, Arnauld, together with Claude Lancelot (1615–95), published the *Port Royal Grammar* [*Grammaire générale et raisonnée*]. The *Logic* remained a textbook into the nineteenth century. The *Grammar* largely dropped from sight until it was "rediscovered" and discussed by Noam Chomsky in his *Cartesian Linguistics* (1966).

Cartesian ideas pervaded both Port Royal books, but in some ways the *Grammar* was the more startling. It not only advanced something like a primitive transformational grammar, but it also suggested that grammar could provide insight into the structure of the human mind. This text actually aimed at a level of abstraction which could begin to constitute a genuine explanation for the grammatical facts. Chomsky finds in the *Grammar* recursive devices which provide for infinite use of the finite means at its disposal. This capacity for a finite set of rules to spin out an infinite set of sentences is a requirement of any adequate grammar. At that point in history, long before work on recursion in the 1930s, the elementary feedback mechanism (i.e. a device which feeds part of its output back to its input enabling it potentially to be repeated ad infinitum) which Arnauld and Lancelot introduced is really a primitive recursive device. It was that step which excited Chomsky. Where Descartes (and later, Malebranche) believed that in geometry the essence of the material world was revealed, so one can read Arnauld as holding that grammar reveals the essence of the mind. Or to put it in a ratio: *grammar is to mind as geometry is to matter.*

Port Royal was the name affixed to a convent and study center as well as to a movement within the French Catholic Church. Arnauld, the members of his very large family (he was the last born in a family of twenty), and the Port Royalists were heavily influenced by the writings of Cornelius Jansen (1585–1638), the Flemish bishop of Ypres. Jansenism was condemned by outsiders as a sort of Catholic Calvinism. Members subscribed to a strict morality and they sought to bring purity to the Church, but some of their theological views, such as those on grace and predestination, caused trouble. Indeed, Cardinal Richelieu suspected that the Port Royalists were troublemakers who might constitute a secret organization capable of interfering with royal power. He blocked Arnauld's advancement, but immediately upon Richelieu's death (1643) Arnauld was made a Doctor of the Sorbonne and ordained a priest. The Jansenists emphasized man's fallen state and the inability of man to gain favor in God's eyes without divine grace. The Pope, however, sought to destroy Port Royal and the Jansenist "heresy" in good measure because the Port Royalists had declared war on the Jesuits and the corrupting influence of their ideas, particularly those ideas which aimed to find an accord between God's grace and his foreknowledge. Arnauld fought the first papal condemnation on behalf of Port Royal by arguing that the offending propositions condemned by the Pope were not in the text of Jansen. The condemnation was in due course amended, at which point Arnauld held that while the propositions now quoted were in the text they were not in the text in the sense in which they had been condemned! It took several years, and several popes, before a condemnation was finally correctly formulated and thus became technically applicable. Arnauld was eventually forced into exile in The Netherlands (he died in Brussels). Even the buildings at Port Royal were leveled.

Arnauld's writings fill several dozen volumes. He wrote extensively on philosophy and theology while much of the time he was the day-to-day leader of an embattled religious movement. He carried on an extended debate with Malebranche over, as will be noted below, Cartesian and Malebranchian ideas. It was often said that Malebranche kept trying to refute Arnauld even after the latter's death! Another philosopher/theologian much influenced by Port Royal is the brilliant mathematician and scientist Blaise Pascal (1623–62). He is sometimes not ranked as a Cartesian, perhaps because of his strongly-held purely religious views, but he was certainly a Cartesian in the sense that he was firmly committed to the mathematical method in both philosophy and science, even if he uttered a few harsh words about Descartes ("we don't think all his philosophy is worth an hour's trouble").

Another philosopher who is not always counted as a Cartesian but who was certainly deeply influenced by him is Baruch de Spinoza (1632–77). Spinoza was born in Amsterdam and raised in its Jewish community. He was once seen as a symbol of opposition to clerical narrow-mindedness because he was excommunicated from his synagogue. On examination, however, the Amsterdam Portuguese–Jewish community seems not to have been as restrictive as it had once been assumed to be. Many members of the congregation were from Spain and Portugal and hence acquainted with European thought and even scholastic philosophy. However, almost three hundred people were excommunicated during the seventeenth century for a wide variety of offenses. Spinoza retained a few friends among the Jewish community and he also found a circle of friends among a creedless and radical Protestant group. He had a modest pension, ground lenses apparently primarily for scientists, and set about writing. Having the advantage of knowing the Talmud and the various relevant "ancient" languages, he began work on what was later to be known as "Bible Criticism." He maintained that ancient biblical material which purported to describe supernatural events should be treated simply as historical material. He subjected such notions as miracles and prophecies to rigorous analysis with the result that he claimed that religion had no positive role except to purvey moral teachings, teachings which would best be taught directly and without the hypocrisy of wrapping the lessons up in myths. Thus Spinoza completely short-circuited the arguments of those committed to the Bible as a revealed text. The Bible was just another book, badly composed at that, reporting on events which occurred long, long ago. Spinoza wrote at a time when prophecy was taken very seriously by the best minds of the period. And scholars often knew Hebrew, Aramaic, and even Arabic. There was much excitement that the Messiah was on the way: for Jews, the first time – for Christians, the second coming. For Christians, the conversion of the Jews received the highest priority since only with their conversion would Christ re-appear. As a result, theologians and other scholars were generally well-acquainted with Jewish texts. There was an almost ecumenical spirit in the air between Christians and Jews as they pored over millennialist texts searching for keys to the date of the arrival of the Messiah. Descartes's close friend, Mersenne, for example, was by no means unusual in his knowledge of Jewish Kabbalistic writings.

Although Spinoza was greatly in Descartes's debt, he parted company with Cartesian ideas in several major ways. He rejected the sceptical option: if one knew, for example, a mathematical proposition, one appreciated that there was no basis for a universal doubt. In his posthumously published *Ethics* (1677), Spinoza explored another dimension of Cartesian philosophy. Whereas Descartes had two substances, mind and matter, Spinoza had but one substance, God, with two attributes – thought and extension. In "popular" philosophical parlance, Spinoza's doctrine is often called psychophysical parallelism. Every event on the mental side is said to have a corresponding material event, and vice versa. On another topic, Spinoza again takes a non-Cartesian line: he rejects free will. The universe is completely determined. When we think we are free, we are living an illusion. The *true* freedom we should aim for is to reach an understanding of the immutable flow of necessary events. Thus Cartesian contingency is rejected, as is Descartes's sharp distinction between truths of essence versus truths of existence. For Spinoza, *ultimately* every truth is an essential truth although it is our ignorance which prevents our seeing the universal necessity in things.

In his *Theologico-Political Treatise* (1670), the only book he published in his lifetime, Spinoza not only wrote about Bible criticism, he also argued for freedom of thought and speech. While he favored freedom of speech "in principle," he carefully circumscribed it so that the state would be free to suppress speech which it took to be subversive. He had a wide circle of friends, strangely enough, among Christian millennialists, among Quakers, and of course among philosophers – including Leibniz.

Leibniz (1646–1716) is another major philosopher whose ideas owe much to Descartes. Leibniz was, like most of the philosophers who followed in Descartes's steps, a brilliant mathematician (Spinoza seems to be the only exception). Indeed, by 1675 Leibniz had formalized the calculus, using the (now) standard rules of differentiation and integration and the dx/f notation. Isaac Newton subsequently presented his own account of the calculus and an extended (and often unpleasant) debate ensued over the priority of their discoveries. Leibniz's courtesy in the matter was not matched by the churlish behavior of Newton and his proteges. Newton, as President of the Royal Society, was judge in his own case!

Leibniz maintained that the world was constituted of monads, spiritual atoms, so to speak, in a monistic (spiritual, i.e. non-dualist) universe. Minds were the pre-eminent atoms and they did not interact with one another. They had "no windows," but they appeared to interact because each atom had a self-contained program by virtue of its own individual concept. Two principles governed Leibniz's metaphysics: the law of non-contradiction, and the principle of sufficient reason, i.e. everything has a reason. According to Leibniz, in every true proposition, the predicate is contained within the subject. This view of true propositions is quite traditional, i.e. the identity principle. In the case of logical truths, the presence of the predicate within the subject is evident. For example, in "a triangle is a three-sided polygon," "three-sided polygon" is contained within the meaning of "triangle". To insert "four-sided" would generate a contradiction. On the other hand, in the case of contingent propositions, the link between the subject and the predicate cannot be discerned by logic. Yet if the proposition is true, even in the case of a contingent proposition, the predicate must be contained within the subject. In those cases the principle of sufficient reason does the work. God, and God alone, has a reason for selecting one predicate for actualization rather than another. This is where the role of monads and their concepts appears. Each monad "reflects," from its own point of view, the entire universe. This seems to mean that all possible predicates are present within the concept of each and every monad. But this does not mean that every possible predicate is actualized, i.e. asserted of the monad's subject. But it does mean that *whatever* predicate is actualized it is singled out from among the infinite possible predicates since they are *all* "in" the subject.

Because of the principle of sufficient reason, Leibniz felt compelled to give a reason for God's having chosen this particular world. Answer: this is the best of all possible worlds, an answer which Voltaire (1694–1778) satirized in his *Candide* (1759). This does not mean, according to Leibniz, that God's choices are necessary. On the contrary, God has freely chosen this world – and that means he has chosen the predicates which are actualized for each and every monad, on the basis of a choice for what is best. The results are *certain*, but they are not *necessary*. God is under no necessity to choose the best, hence the principle of sufficient reason does not collapse into the principle of non-contradiction – although critics have often argued that it did.

The greatest seventeenth-century Cartesian is Nicolas Malebranche (1638–1715). After studying philosophy and theology he became a priest in the Oratory, an order founded by Descartes's one-time spiritual advisor, Cardinal Pierre de Berulle (1575–1629). It was a politically delicate time for the Order. Thanks to its founder, it was strongly Augustinian. But it had to be cautious in order to avoid being called either Cartesian or Jansenist. As a student Malebranche became completely disenchanted with the scholastic method of disputation. His encounter with Descartes's *Treatise on Man* revolutionized his thinking. The first three books of his *Search after Truth*[27] *[De la recherche de la vérité]* were published in 1674, the second three in 1675. Because various passages in the *Search* caused difficulties, he published, in accordance with the policy of replying to objections and queries which Descartes had inaugurated, seventeen *Clarifications [éclaircissements]* in 1678.

Malebranche, like Augustine before him, accepts *cogito ergo sum*. But unlike Descartes he rejects the demon deceiver, because if one lets such a sceptical doubt corrode mathematical truths, there is no firmer place from which one can restore the path to truth. Secondly, Malebranche rejects innate ideas. He agrees with both Augustine and Descartes that the objects of real knowledge are not derived from sense experience. But he finds innate ideas an inefficient way for God to guarantee the foundation of real knowledge. Rather, "we see all things in God." We each have access to the single set of eternal ideas, i.e. those which are the constituents of the eternal truths. This helps explain how two mathematicians, separated by both time and space, can ponder the very same problem. Malebranche takes Descartes to have drawn a sharp "ontological" distinction between concepts (such as the ideas of mathematics) and our purely mental sensations. Thus one set of eternal ideas is "in" God while as many particular sensations as may arise in human minds are *not* "in" God.

Like Descartes, Malebranche does not deny that we have sensations but he denies, again like Descartes, that these sensations constitute knowledge. Knowledge, as Plato had articulated long ago, must be (1) of a real (i.e. independent) thing, and (2) it must be infallible. Sensations, being in "the flux," are disqualified on the first count although first person sensory judgments have generally been taken to be infallible, at least in the sense that no one else seems to be in a position to correct them. Like Descartes, Malebranche rejects abstractionism from sense data as a way of furnishing the mind. Given that no relation of resemblance holds between perceptions and so-called external objects (recall Sextus and Montaigne on whether the portrait of Socrates resembles him – if one has never seen Socrates), the very notion of abstraction is non-sensical. And again like Descartes, and unlike Spinoza, he subscribes to a sharp essence/existence distinction. Malebranche argues at length for what he calls *intelligible extension*. This is the set of eternal ideas which make up the essence of the material world, and which he seems to take to be an algebraic representation of geometry in order to drive home the point that these Ideas do not stand in a relation of resemblance to sensibly perceived things. Again, like Descartes, when one knows this mathematical domain one knows all possible material worlds in the sense that there can be no material object which is not comprehended by geometry. But Malebranche breaks with Descartes over minds. We are aware of our thoughts and our sensations, but we totally lack insight into the essence of the mind. There is no, so to speak, *intelligible thought* parallel to the set of ideas which illuminates the material world. There is no mathematical psychology on the analogue of geometry. Nor, he believes, can grammar (e.g. of the sort found in the *Port Royal Grammar*) fill that requirement. We are aware of the *existence* of the world of mind since we experience it, but lack a grasp of its *essence*; we know the essence of the material world, but not its existence. Indeed, despite the range of experiences we now have, there may be (for all we know) no existent material world! The only reason we are entitled to believe that there is a material world is that its creation is divinely revealed in Genesis.

As a consequence of the sharp essence/existence distinction which Malebranche takes over from Descartes, such formal deductions as we perform belong in the domain of essence. An appreciation of the pervasive use of the distinction (even, as noted above, extending to the titles of the fifth and sixth *Meditations*) makes it virtually impossible to formulate a "super-deductivist" interpretation. For neither Descartes nor Malebranche can we deduce "matters of fact." Take any existential claim, i.e. any matter of fact; its denial may be false but it is not logically contradictory. Thus "This triangle is red," may in fact be true. And although its denial, "This triangle is not red," may be false, it is not contradictory. In a totally deductivist world (in the fashion of what I have called the "super-deductivist" model), "This triangle is not red" would not only be false, it would be contradictory. Spinoza appears to be the only person in the Cartesian tradition who is a radical deductivist, one for whom not only purely logically necessary claims (e.g. a triangle has three sides) but also all matters of fact statements are logically necessary. Even Spinoza, however, attenuates the force of his claim by saying that it is because of ignorance that we fail to see the logical connections that make even matter of fact claims logically necessary. Neither Descartes nor Malebranche accept Spinoza's claim. For them, existential claims, i.e. statements about empirical facts, never possess logical certainty. The line between essence and existence is never breached. Matters of fact are products of God's will – and we have no access to God's will beyond chronicling what happens on a day-to-day basis. Moreover, given that both Descartes and Malebranche subscribe to the doctrine that God is engaged in continuous re-creation of the world, we are presented with another basis for the denial of necessary connections within our world.

What drives the "super-deductivist" reading in the face of so much counter evidence? My guess is that since Descartes and Malebranche accept proofs of God's *existence*, the critics believe that the essence/existence distinction has been violated and so they think that if God's existence can be logically established by deduction, consistency ought to require that the deductivist argument extend to everything. But recall how careful Descartes is to say that proofs of God's existence constitute a special case because God is a special case. Only in God do essence and existence coincide. In the mid-eighteenth century, David Hume (1711–76) made much of the essence/existence distinction, although he called it "relations of ideas" versus "matters of fact". But he didn't think much of substances, mental, material, or divine: "We have no perfect idea of anything but of a perception. A substance is entirely different from a perception. We have, therefore, no idea of a substance" (*Treatise of Human Nature* [I, iv, § 5]). Hume's account leaves little room for a conceptually coherent analysis of a deity. Hume may have liked Malebranche's account of non-necessary causal connections but he considered that making God a causal agent was unintelligible. Treating God as a special case hardly helps if God has already been ruled out as a causal agent.

Malebranche was widely read in his lifetime. By 1700 the *Search* had been twice rendered into English. John Locke felt compelled to write two essays attacking Malebranche, largely because he feared (correctly) that "seeing all things in God" would be taken as a rationalist alternative to Locke's empiricist model. George Berkeley (1685–1753), the second of the so-called "British Empiricists" (Locke–Berkeley–Hume), was nevertheless a defender of innate ideas. He was often considered by his contemporaries as a Malebranchist. David Hume, traditionally ranked as an empiricist, was nevertheless a careful reader of Malebranche's writings and seems to have been influenced by the non-necessary quality of Malebranche's causal connections. For both Descartes and, more obviously for Malebranche, God is the *only* true cause and there are no real secondary causes. However, God's actions, the causes he may generate, are functions of his will, not his intellect. Once again one sees how crucial the sharp distinction between essence and existence is for Descartes and Malebranche. We have no conceptual grasp of God's will. In the domain of existence, all we can do is monitor the empirical data and tabulate the events without the benefit of logical links. That is a consequence of the radical asymmetry between essence and existence, between God's Ideas and the choices he makes. To repeat: we have no access to whatever principles, if any, lie behind God's choices. Note however, that Malebranche and Arnauld fought for years over the correct interpretation of Descartes's distinction between ideas taken as conceptual entities, and ideas taken as sensations.

Descartes was also a major influence on Pierre Bayle (1647–1706), the "Philosopher of Rotterdam." Bayle does not always appear in lists of philosophers, which is unfortunate, because he was a major disseminator of philosophical ideas as well as being an original thinker in his own right. Those eighteenth-century writers who were hostile to organized religion often described his arguments as the "Arsenal of the Enlightenment" but they generally ignored his more properly philosophical contributions. Only in the last forty years has he begun to receive the attention he deserves.

A recent review of some new studies of Bayle as a philosopher begins (although reflecting a somewhat stronger judgment than I would use!): "Why do professional philosophers spend so much time on Descartes and so little time on Pierre Bayle, when Bayle was clearly the better philosopher?"[28]

Born into a French Calvinist family, Bayle was eventually obliged to flee France (like tens of thousands of other Protestants) even before the limited religious toleration granted members of the French Reformed Church under the provisions of the Edict of Nantes (1598) was revoked in 1685. However, before that momentous event there were still Protestant academies. One of the most important was at Saumur and it became, in 1665, the first French Protestant academy to appoint a Cartesian to its faculty. It was an hospitable environment for Cartesianism since the nearby College of the Oratorians had already welcomed both Cartesian and later Malebranchian ideas. The physician Louis De La Forge (1632–66), probably also another La Flèche graduate, lived in Saumur and while there wrote his *Treatise on the Spirit of Man* (1666), a text based on Descartes's theory of mind. Five years later, Saumur's "star" Protestant Cartesian, Jean-Robert Chouet (1642–1731), accepted a professorship at Geneva, and so Cartesianism was propagated within Calvin's own city.

It was at Geneva that the young Bayle met teachers who were striving to produce a synthesis of Calvinism and the "new" (i.e. Cartesian and Malebranchian) philosophy. By the 1660s Descartes did not universally strike fear into Dutch Calvinist theologians, although some French Calvinists were often as distressed by Cartesian ideas as some of their Dutch confreres were. But the theologians at Saumur took a different line. Virtually from the outset, rather than being frightened by Descartes, they welcomed his ideas and sought to incorporate them into their versions of Calvinism. As a result, many previously sacrosanct elements of Calvinist theology were subjected to careful philosophical scrutiny. This included analyses of faith in the light of natural reason.[29] As Descartes himself had discovered, the question of whether reason imposed constraints of rationality on matters of faith was very sensitive. From the very outset there had been a strong strand of rationalism within Calvinism. Cartesianism provided that strand with a framework within which it could be made more intelligible and then developed. Bayle was an observer of these developments at first hand and what he learned he carried with him when he took up a post as a professor of philosophy at the Ecole Illustre in Rotterdam.

Living relatively comfortably in a refugee community, Bayle found time to write a number of influential books. While seeking to show that religious toleration was a consequence not only of Christian teaching, properly understood, Bayle produced a very extended and subtle examination of the notions of conscience and of mental privacy. The end result was a virtually absolutist defense of religious toleration, as extreme as the seventeenth or any other century seems to have produced. Bayle made use of Cartesianism to apply the principle of clear and distinct ideas within his argument and he relied heavily on dualism. Mental privacy, the view that our minds were not exposed to examination by anyone other than God, was something he used against his more bigoted friends and neighbors within the Orthodox (Reformed) community. But the text which secured his wider fame in the Republic of Letters was his *Historical and Critical Dictionary*, the first edition of which appeared in 1697 and a second and much enlarged edition in 1702. Two English editions soon appeared.

The arguments on behalf of religious toleration included one which particularly scandalized both religious and political figures. In a number of texts Bayle demonstrated, at least to the satisfaction of many, the astonishing claim, astonishing to his confreres at least, that there is no logical tie between one's religious views and the morality exhibited in one's behavior. There is no logical impediment to postulating a moral society of atheists. *Were there a necessary connection between religion and morality, such a postulation would be contradictory*. Bayle makes his case by examining a wide range of examples: from Roman times, from Islamic behavior, and – of course – by probing the depths of corruption in Christian states. His point is that there is no evidence to be found in history to show that so-called religious societies are necessarily moral. Traditionally, states impose official religions on their populations in order to guarantee civil peace. When extraordinary means are taken to bring about conversions to an established religion, far from guaranteeing civil peace, the historical evidence shows that one puts it at risk. Moreover, the price is high because one creates hypocritical members of the established religion. And such coercion, known as "forcing consciences," amounts to violating mental privacy. More is at stake:

> For if objective knowledge arose out of freedom for speculative thought, society must positively protect the conditions which made such trial and error possible. The matter at issue therefore was about government, not religion. If the society in which scholars offered free criticism of one another's conjectures was as orderly as the society which forbade it, then free communities had a better chance of acquiring knowledge and making improvements than communities which feared criticism and suppressed dissent.[30]

The *Dictionary* contains articles on all sorts of figures from the Greek and Latin classical world, many of the heroes of the Reformation, and a number of philosophers. Each article contains textual material to which are appended footnotes ("Remarks"). The interesting material is generally in the notes. This makes it very difficult to read Bayle systematically. The *Dictionary* is, however, never dull. There are all sorts of ribald stories slipped into the most abstruse discussions. These guaranteed him an audience, but also the opposition of the more puritanical leaders of the Reformed Church.

Article *Mammillarians*, is a case in point. They are described as:

> A sect among the Anabaptists. I am not sure of the date when this new schism developed, but it is said that Haarlem is the birthplace of this subdivision. It owes its origins to the liberty a young man took by putting his hand on the breast of a girl whom he loved and wanted to marry. This touch became known to the Church, which deliberated on the punishments the delinquent ought to suffer. Some claimed that he ought to be excommunicated; others said that his fault was pardonable and therefore they would never agree to his excommunication. The dispute grew so hot that it led to a total rupture between

the contending parties. Those who had favored being indulgent
toward the young man were called Mammillarians ...

This short article concludes with some stories which have a titillat-
ing quality. But there is also another dimension to the article. Bayle
is calling attention to a pervasive feature of human associations. We
have a remarkable capacity for finding ways and means for distinguishing ourselves from the other members of our group. Bayle had
observed at first hand with what ease churches were forever splitting
into ever smaller groups. Feeling oppressed by our social organizations we seem to relish the process of dichotomization. The natural
end of this process would of course be that each person constitutes a
"minority of one," that is, taking the self to be a Cartesian "atom," to
use (see p.97) Charles Taylor's term.

In his article *David*, Bayle recounts the crimes and sex life of the
biblical David, always against the background chorus that David
was "a man after God's own heart." Another theme which greatly
irritated the ecclesiastical authorities was the discussion of
Pyrrhonism. There is no overt sign that Bayle has Descartes's
demon deceiver in mind, but Bayle does cite the Cartesians (*Pyrrho*,
Remark B) among the philosophers who brought us to see that "no
good philosopher any longer doubts that the sceptics were right to
maintain that the qualities of bodies that strike our senses are only
appearances." Bayle then asks: "Does God deceive mankind with
regard to colors? If he deceives them about this, what prevents him
from so doing with regard to extension?" He seems to hold in the
article *Pyrrho* that by setting certain articles of the Christian religion (e.g. the Trinitarian doctrine that three persons [God, Son, and
Holy Spirit] are unified as one) over against purely evident mathematical truths, one can demonstrate the *falsity* of those evident
truths (provided, of course, that truth-priority has been given to the
Christian principles). Popkin, in his comment on Remark B (of
Pyrrho) writes that Bayle "is going beyond any previous sceptic in
challenging the contention that *l'évidence* is the criterion of truth,
by suggesting that a proposition can have *l'évidence* and yet be
known to be false." This was a step no other sceptic (e.g. Sextus,
Huet, or Gassendi) made. He was however, amusingly dogmatic

when he reportedly said: "I am a good Protestant and in the full strength of that term, because from the bottom of my soul, I protest everything that is said, and everything that is done."

Throughout the *Dictionary*, Bayle takes up philosophical, mainly Cartesian/Malebranchian, themes. He discusses at length Simon Foucher's criticism of Malebranche. Foucher takes Malebranche (and Descartes) to be subscribing to the primary/secondary quality distinction along something approaching Lockean lines. That is, our ideas of the secondary qualities do not *resemble* real qualities in things whereas ideas of primary qualities do. But, or so the discussions went, if variations in sense experience lead us to say that ideas, e.g. of heat and color, do not resemble qualities in things, then (as Bayle argues in *Pyrrho* and elsewhere) the same should hold for the primary qualities. They too vary. To repeat, what the "variations in sense experience" claim suggests is that our visual perception of an object with respect to *both* the so-called primary and secondary qualities varies with the state of our perceptual system. For example, we may have jaundice, or astigmatism, etc. This moves the argument in the direction of saying there is no way of telling whether our ideas of secondary qualities, no less our ideas of primary qualities, map on to anything in the world, and hence that there may be nothing but our ideas, an option actually taken up a few years later by George Berkeley (1685–1753). As suggested above, neither Descartes nor Malebranche subscribed to the "resemblance" doctrine, but that detail was lost in the polemics of the day. And the "reduction" of the primary to the secondary qualities became the stock-in-trade for generations of philosophers. Few people read Foucher. Everyone read Bayle's interpretation of Foucher's argument.[31]

Bayle was fascinated by an issue which ties into the primary/secondary quality discussion: the nature of extension and the matter of its divisibility. A delightful formulation of the divisibility problem is to be found in the article *Zeno of Elea*. The classical statement is to be found in Aristotle. However, neither Aristotle nor his followers were ever able to provide a universally satisfactory resolution of the difficulties Zeno advanced. Bayle argues that Aristotle plays with a distinction between real and potential infinitives but that his effort fails. There are four paradoxes: two directed against the assumption that space is finitely divisible and two against infinite divisibility. Bayle formulates and then reformulates the paradoxes again and again. It is clear that Bayle finds the paradoxes a marvelous testimony to the existence of a Pyrrhonian core at the very heart of the intelligibility of our universe – and at the same time he finds the paradoxes hilarious.

The motion of an arrow in flight is impossible. This is, we might say, a cinematographic picture of the motion with the camera set at one frame per indivisible moment. But the arrow must, by hypothesis, move. How does it move from one frame to the next? It seems that motion actually occurs between the frames. But that is impossible. So finite divisibility leads to absurdity. It seems that one is driven to postulating more frames. So the second option takes us to infinite divisibility. What moves, says Bayle, must pass from one place to another. But now it emerges that there are an infinite number of parts between any two points. Hence, an infinite time will be required since an infinite number of points must be traversed. By hypothesis one cannot skip over points.

The third paradox is perhaps the best known: Achilles and the Tortoise. A tortoise starts the race twenty paces ahead of Achilles, who runs twenty times as fast as the tortoise. So, when Achilles strides ahead twenty paces and reaches the place where the tortoise had been, the tortoise has moved ahead one pace. Achilles then moves ahead one pace and thus reaches the place where the tortoise had been. But the tortoise has already moved ahead one twentieth of a pace. When Achilles then moves ahead one twentieth of a pace, the tortoise has already moved ahead a twentieth of a twentieth, etc., ad infinitum. Given infinite divisibility, Achilles will apparently never catch the tortoise! Bayle's delightful formulation of the fourth paradox deserves to be quoted in full:

> Imagine a table of four ells, and take two bodies of four ells also, one of wood, the other of stone. Let the table be immoveable and let it support the piece of wood with the length of two ells to the west. Let the piece of stone be to the east, and let it only touch the edge of the

table. Let it move on this table toward the west, and let it travel two ells in a half hour. It will then become contiguous to the piece of wood. Let us suppose that they only meet at their edges, and in such a way that the motion of the one toward the west does not hinder the motion of the other toward the east. At the moment that they become contiguous, let the piece of wood begin to move eastward, while the other [i.e. the stone] continues to move westward. Let them move at equal speeds. In half an hour the piece of stone will have traversed the entire table. It will then have traversed a space of four ells in an hour, that is the entire surface of the table. Now the piece of wood in half an hour has gone through a similar space of four ells, *since it has touched the edges of the entire extension of the piece of stone* [my emphasis]. It is therefore the case that two bodies, which move with equal speed, traverse the same distance, one in half an hour, the other in an hour. Therefore, an hour and a half an hour are equal times, which is contradictory.[32]

Bayle moves on to offer a range of arguments against extension. He applies this to atoms. The notion of an extended indivisible atom is, as Descartes had noted, incoherent. If the atom has a left side and a right side, a top and a bottom, it has parts. Bayle's aim is to establish that extension, according to Descartes the essential property of the material world, can not be understood to map directly on to the so-called real external world. As has been repeatedly noted above, Descartes provides no transition or means to link extension (as essence) to existent things. The problem of mapping mathematical models on to the world had already been a source of distress even for the ancient Pythagoreans since it suggested that we could not grasp the world with precision. If extension is understood to be composed of mathematical points, or of atoms, or of infinitely divisible parts, the difficulties are overwhelming. We are thus entitled to say that extension is impossible and that it has only ideal existence, i.e. existence only in our minds. We must conclude that there are things which the mind of man cannot understand. Accordingly, "is it not manifestly sinning against reason to refuse to believe in the marvelous effects of the almighty power of God, which is incomprehensible in itself, because our mind cannot understand them."[33]

At the heading of the very next Remark, *Zeno* (remark H), Bayle writes: "The proofs that reason furnishes us of the existence of matter are not evident enough to furnish a good demonstration" (Popkin's translation). Bayle then discusses Malebranche's view that "Descartes has not found any other unshakable foundation than the argument that God would deceive us if there were no bodies. But [Malebranche] claims that this argument cannot pass for a demonstrative one." Malebranche,[34] as reported by Bayle, holds that Descartes must demonstrate with geometric rigor not only that there is a God and that he is not a deceiver, but also that he has actually created bodies. But we know there are bodies only by faith, and not by strict demonstration. Thus Malebranche rejects Descartes's proof that God would be a deceiver if no bodies were to exist in reality, although whether Descartes's account at the end of the sixth *Meditation* really constitutes such a proof has been challenged above. As already noted, Berkeley, very familiar with the arguments of Descartes, Malebranche, and Bayle, took the lack of a "proof" of the existence of matter seriously and sought actually to *prove* the non-existence of matter. Questions about "proofs" for the "existence of the external world" are often thought to appear for the very first time thanks to seventeenth-century Cartesianism and that accordingly, no variant of the "sin of idealism" in the sense of a doubt about the existence of the external world is said to appear in medieval or ancient philosophy. On the face of it, that is a remarkable claim inasmuch as the Pyrrhonians seem to have doubted so many things. So we should perhaps not be surprised to find Sextus (*Adv. Math.* VII, 366) saying "all external objects are non-evident and on this account unknowable by us."

Many of the articles concern the problem of evil. This is a topic Bayle was deeply troubled by, in no small measure because his brother had been killed by French Catholic authorities, probably only because he was Bayle's brother. He was intrigued by (but dissatisfied with) Leibniz's "solution." And he wrote about the Manicheans and their good–evil dualism. But at bottom, he was worried, as was Descartes, about the role of reason in relation to faith. It is a topic which got him into serious trouble with his fellow members of the Reformed community in Rotterdam. Was Bayle a serious believer? Was he a secret atheist – or perhaps not so secret? In the Third Clarification, which he was obliged to append to the *Dictionary*, he wrote:

> Every dispute about the question of religion's prerogatives ought to be rejected from the very first word. No one ought to be allowed to examine whether it is necessary to believe what God orders us to believe. This ought to be accepted as a first principle in matters of religion … Theologians should not be ashamed to admit that they cannot enter a contest with such antagonists [philosophers], and that they do not want to expose the Gospel truths to such an attack. The bark of Jesus Christ is not made for sailing on this stormy sea, but for taking shelter from this tempest in the haven of faith. It has pleased the Father, the Son, and the Holy Ghost, Christians ought to say, to lead us by the path of faith, and not by the path of knowledge or disputation. They are our teachers and our directors. We cannot lose our way with such guides. And reason itself commands us to prefer them to its direction.[35]

There were other major philosophical themes, for example, the matter of historical truth. While it is true that Bayle was a sceptic about many things, he was also a committed historian and often devoted extraordinary efforts to track down "facts." Elisabeth Labrousse maintains that Bayle transposed the Cartesian method and its concern with principles of procedure to historical investigations.[36] That is, Bayle was self-consciously Cartesian/Malebranchian in the application of both methodic doubt and the quest for evidence (clarity and distinctness) *in historical matters*. As has often been noted, this generates tension between Bayle's application of Pyrrhonism to scientific and philosophical ideas versus his firm commitment to moral principles. Also, following the concerns of both Descartes and Malebranche, in an article *Rorarius* he discussed Leibniz's attempt to resolve puzzles over God's role in causation. At issue was whether we, in addition to God, were causal agents. For Descartes and Malebranche God was the only real agent in all contexts. The resultant doctrine was known as "occasionalism." I don't move my arm myself; God moves it. Leibniz substituted the doctrine of "pre-established harmony." The spiritual entities which comprise the world are like clocks which are so structured that they seem to interact with one another but really are only programmed to create that appearance. For example, I might be programmed to push someone, and that person would in turn be programmed to be pushed. There is thus *apparent* causal interaction between the two people, but no *real* causal interaction. Bayle thought Leibniz was a genius but he found this doctrine just a clever variant of occasionalism since God was still the only real cause in the system.

"There is nothing deep down inside us except what we have put there ourselves"

Hostility towards Descartes steadily increased in both breadth and depth from the seventeenth century to the present. Here are a few words on three different sorts of criticism, criticisms which are less concerned with precise arguments than with more general considerations. Perhaps the most famous post-World War II philosophical attack on Cartesian dualism came from Gilbert Ryle (1900–76). His *The Concept of Mind*[37] dominated anti-Cartesianism for a generation. One chapter, "Descartes' Myth" seeks totally to unravel Descartes's dualism. This is how he understands Cartesian minds:

> Minds are not in space, nor are their operations subject to mechanical laws. The workings of one mind are not witnessable by other observers; its career is private. Only I can take direct cognisance of the states and processes of my own mind. A person therefore lives through two collateral histories, one consisting of what happens in and to his body, the other consisting of what happens in and to his mind. The first is public, the second private. (p. 11)

Lacking direct access to "other minds," we must infer, on the basis of the behavior of others, that their private mental lives are similar to our own. Ryle considers this account of the mental to be absurd and he speaks of the "official [i.e. Cartesian] theory as 'the dogma of the Ghost in the

95

Machine' " (pp. 15–16). He adds: "Because, as is true, a person's thinking, feeling and purposive doing cannot be described solely in the idioms of physics, chemistry and physiology, therefore they must be described in counterpart idioms." To make that philosophical move is to make what Ryle calls a category-mistake.

> Still unwittingly adhering to the grammar of mechanics, [Descartes] tried to avert disaster by describing minds in what was merely an obverse vocabulary. The workings of minds had to be described by the mere negatives of the specific descriptions given to bodies; they are not in space, they are not motions, they are not modifications of matter, they are not accessible to public observation. Minds are not bits of clockwork, they are just bits of not-clockwork. (p. 20)

Thus Ryle sought to treat mind-body dualism as a gross philosophical error, the product of what he called a category-mistake, in this case, the error of attributing substance status to mind exactly parallel to the substance status of matter. Ryle successfully tilted the discussion a bit more towards materialism and to behaviorism/empiricism, and it remained there for more than a generation. Ryle's arguments seek to show that all mind-talk can be dismissed because despite appearances, mind-talk does not call into existence a special substance, i.e. a *mind*. Mind-talk can be translated, without loss of meaning, into talk about human behavior. Ryle provides one way to challenge Cartesianism.

Here is a second sort of anti-Cartesianism. It is the anti-foundationalist option. There is a very large list of recent publications on the subject, but only two items will be discussed. In his contribution ("Overcoming Epistemology") to *After Philosophy: End or Transformation,* Charles Taylor (1931–) says that the epistemological tradition to be "overcome" holds that "knowledge is to be seen as correct representation of an independent reality."[38] He names as major critics of this tradition: Hegel (1770–1831), Heidegger (1889–1976), Merleau-Ponty (1908–61), and Wittgenstein (1889–1951). He maintains that the decisive shift in focus is that from trying to locate an independent foundation of knowledge to a recognition that we are always agents in the world and hence that a total "disengagement" from it is impossible. He puts it this way:

Foundationalism is undermined, because you can't go on digging under our ordinary representations to uncover further, more basic representations. What you get underlying our representations is not further representations but rather a certain grasp of the world that we have as agents in it. This shows the whole epistemological construal of knowledge is mistaken. (p. 477)

Throughout his career Charles Taylor, Canada's best known philosopher, has been a severe critic of Descartes. His attack on epistemological foundations and on what he takes to be more basic, representationalism, and hence his global attack on Descartes, has an immediate political goal. Thus Taylor attacks representationalism because he sees it as sending us on a quest for "foundations." But we do not encounter the world in that way. We are not, he holds, peeling away appearances of things intending to find bedrock on which genuine knowledge can be constructed. We can't encounter such independent elements. And we can't because, he says, we are always agents in the world. We can't reach and then hold on to a Really Real and independent entity. If there were an independent foundation, we would never be able to grasp it, we could never be in touch with it. As for the world, we have a grasp of it because we are agents in that world. That is what it means to be an agent.

Augustine was the inventor of the argument we know as the "cogito", because Augustine was the first to make the first-person standpoint fundamental to our search for the truth ... But Descartes gives Augustinian inwardness a radical twist and takes it in quite a new direction, which has also been epoch-making. The change might be described by saying that Descartes situates the moral source within us ... The idea that there may be no legitimate authority is obviously too dangerous to be tolerable. The doctrine of the divine right of kings provided an alternative to contract theory in the seventeenth-century ... Divine right assumed atomism [i.e. taking each of us to be Cartesian selves, to be discreet "atoms"]; That is, it took for granted that there were no natural relations of authority among men, and it then argued that only a special grant of divine power could avoid the chaos of anarchy. The earlier doctrines had assumed that human communities had authority ... [39]

Taylor's argument against Descartes is not narrowly abstract. Writing on the subject of the contemporary Quebec/Canada scene he blames the "hyper-Cartesian visions" of the late Canadian prime minister Pierre-Eliot Trudeau and of the late Quebec premier René Lévesque for undermining the old Canadian "two-nation" ideology and hence with contributing to the current (and continuing) Canadian constitutional crisis.[40] My suspicion is that anti-Cartesian and pro-communitarian views merge to give support to a philosopher's belief in a nationalist doctrine of identity. In that way, the nationalism drives the philosophy and not the other way round. It is also supported by his anti-foundationalism. We construct our identities without the benefit of anything more fundamental upon which they can be based. And the (nationalist) identities we construct have the "untouchable" status they have because to protect those identities we destroyed any potentially threatening authority philosophy might have had. We eliminate the atom-self of Descartes and then discover that a community forms the pseudo-foundation in our foundationless world. Without foundations, there is no way to evaluate communities, or to sustain a critical standpoint, or to escape from whatever structure a given community has imposed upon us.

The well-known contemporary American philosopher, Richard Rorty (1931–), another anti-foundationalist, has written in a somewhat similar vein in the same *After Philosophy* volume:

> There is nothing deep down inside us except what we have put there ourselves, no criterion that we have not created in the course of creating a practice, no standard of rationality that is not an appeal to such a criterion, no rigorous argumentation that is not obedience to our own conventions. (p. 60)

This is anti-foundationalism with a vengeance. It is not directed exclusively at Descartes. It is rather a frontal attack on all forms of realism, whether in science, philosophy, ethics, or politics. Nor is it simply an expression of "cultural relativism." The assertion that "there are no standards," at least with respect to ethical, anthropological, or political claims, is probably, in one form or another, as old as recorded history. But when Rorty maintains that there is "no criterion that we have not created in the course of creating a practice," he is undercutting the very possibility of, for example, a human *nature*. Talk about innate ideas, talk about universal moral principles, even talk about so-called "truths" of logic and mathematics, all such things lack any "foundations." Obviously, this cuts at the very heart of Cartesianism. Unlike Rorty and his friends among the postmodernists, Sextus Empiricus and the Pyrrhonians were extremely careful in discussing whether their own "arguments" against the dogmatists were subject to, i.e. reflected back on, their own "apparent" criticisms. Unlike the Pyrrhonian sceptics, the postmodernists are, paradoxically, dogmatic about their own pseudo-sceptical and relativistic arguments.

It is very difficult to make sense of the relativism which characterizes much of postmodernist thought. It is usually driven by attempts to be Politically Correct in one or another domain. In the first instance there seem to have been concerns that each "culture" was a thing in itself and that Western thought was eroding and destroying native cultures. The defense of native cultures took the form of maintaining that the logical means used to "understand" other cultures were in fact vehicles for destroying them. This has led to some strange consequences, from claiming that the law of contradiction is itself culture-bound, to claims about how the structure of the world is dependent on the structure of the language we use to talk about that world. The notion that all humans have a common language faculty and a shared Universal Grammar, as many modern linguists maintain, is viewed as one more instance of Western cultural imperialism. There are even strange arguments which seem to have as consequences that the sciences developed by so-called primitive peoples are "just as good" as ours. How this works for mathematics is not obvious.

As for logic proper, it is sometimes talked about as phallo-logical thinking. That is, it is said to reflect the efforts of males to establish power and control over our thought-processes in such a way as systematically to exclude women. It seems to be one thing to hold that the curriculum in university literary departments pays too much heed to the "dead, white males" and another to assert that only women can write about women, only members of a given ethnic/racial group can write about members of that group, only gays, only transgender folk, or only, say, ethnic Germans, possess the sensibility to write about the respective groups. Presumably, it should follow that only readers with the "right" sensibilities can intelligently read such material and only teachers with the "right" sensibilities can "grade" student papers. Although what it means to "grade" or evaluate in this context is never made clear. Or worse: what can it mean to say that something "follows" from something else when logic is itself viewed as an imperialist/sexist construct? The answer usually provided is that logic, given that there are no longer any "foundations" to which an appeal might be made, is nothing but an expression of raw power in the hands of an elite. How one scales power and how one characterizes the limits of an elite, how one even tallies the numbers of members, without the use of arguments, logic, and mathematics is unclear.

Ryle represents one modern approach to, and attack upon, Descartes. But both Rorty and Taylor move the argument forward. They may be understood as giving a set of reasons for opposing Descartes's arguments. They take Descartes's arguments seriously. They see dangerous social and political consequences from those arguments. They appear to be prepared to accept any paradoxes which might follow from opposing Descartes by advancing a "foundationless" philosophy. However, many modern discussions of the mind–body problem need hardly mention Descartes. In recent years there has been tremendous interest in the brain as a biological entity and an effort to demonstrate that the methods of modern science can dispose of that mystery of the mind inherited from Descartes.

Noam Chomsky has long been puzzled that many commentators forget what Isaac Newton says about contact mechanics. And he continues to be perplexed that the point is often ignored:

> The crucial [Newtonian] discovery was that bodies do not exist. It is common to ridicule the idea of the "ghost in the machine" (as in Gilbert Ryle's influential work, for example). But this misses the point. Newton exorcised the machine, leaving the ghost intact. Furthermore, nothing has replaced the machine ... There is also no coherent notion of material, physical, and so on. Hence there is no

mind–body problem, no question about reduction of the mental to the physical, or even unification of the two domains. The contemporary orthodoxies seem unintelligible, along with the efforts to refute them. Advocates and critics are in the same (sinking) boat, and no reconciliation is needed, or possible.[41]

The philosopher John Searle (1932–)[42] takes the discussion about rationalism and the nature of the human mind in a very different direction from either Chomsky or Ryle or the anti-foundationalists: "If we had an adequate science of the brain, an account of the brain that would give causal explanations of consciousness in all its forms and varieties, and if we overcame our conceptual mistakes, no mind–body problem would remain." Searle does not think we are close to that point, but the dream lives on. Galen Strawson[43] is a committed monist (that is, someone for whom there is only one sort of substance), but he grants that materialists must "admit that they don't have a fully adequate idea of what the physical is or what sort of thing the brain is." And as I noted above, Chomsky maintains that there is no mind–body problem. "For there to be a mind–body problem, there has to be some characterization of body, and Newton eliminated the last conception of body anybody had."[44] Horgan paraphrases what he reports Chomsky told him in an interview: "Newton's own theory of gravity, which showed that objects can influence each other in non-mechanistic ways, actually *shattered* the materialist worldview."

Chomsky has been saying these things for more than an academic generation, but various groups have soldiered on. First, the Artificial Intelligence (AI) people who take the human brain to be a computational device and seek to replicate the brain electronically. It is apparently assumed that if they were successful, it would yield some insight into how the human mind actually works. Hence the defenders of AI were delighted when a computer program beat the world's best chess player. On the other hand, the Oxford mathematician, Roger Penrose (1931–), has argued against the computational model on the ground that a computer is constrained by the proofs which Kurt Gödel advanced in the 1930s concerning what computations could and could NOT establish. Penrose writes:

What Gödel tells us is that no system of computational rules can characterise the properties of the *natural numbers*. Despite the fact that there is no computational way of characterising the natural numbers, any child knows what they are. All you do is to show the child different numbers of objects ... and after a while they can abstract the notion of natural number from these particular instances of it. You do not give the child a set of computational rules – what you are doing is enabling the child to "understand" what natural numbers are. I would say that the child is able to make some kind of "contact" with the Platonic world of mathematics ... Somehow, the natural numbers are already "there", existing somewhere in the Platonic world and we have access to that world through our ability to be aware of things. If we were simply mindless computers, we would not have that ability.[45]

Descartes and Malebranche would be delighted with this Platonistic account of the "home" for the natural numbers. Malcolm Longair explains that for Penrose, abstract mathematics cannot be programmed on a digital computer.

Such a computer cannot discover mathematical theorems in the way that human mathematicians do ... Roger [Penrose] interprets this to mean that the process of mathematical thinking, and by extension all thinking and conscious behaviour, are carried out by "non-computational means" ... Because of the central importance of this result for his general argument, he devoted over half of *Shadows of the Mind* to showing that his interpretation of Gödel's Theorem was watertight.[46]

Although Penrose rejects computational models of mind, and is a Platonist, he is not a dualist. Instead, he argues that a scientific understanding of the nature of mind takes us into physics, specifically into quantum theory.

Philosophers have been arguing about the philosophical implications of Gödel's (and slightly later, Turing's) results since the 1930s. So it is not surprising to find Chalmers (1966–)[47] writing: "I think it is fair to say that the case that Gödelian limitations do not apply to humans has never been convincingly made [e.g. by Penrose]." Yet in his penultimate paragraph, Chalmers says:

I resisted mind–body dualism for a long time, but I have now come to the point where I accept it, not just as the only tenable view but as a satisfying view in its own right. It is always possible that I am confused, or that there is a new and radical possibility that I have overlooked; but I can comfortably say that I think dualism is very likely true. I have also raised the possibility of a kind of panpsychism. Like mind–body dualism, this is initially counterintuitive, but the counterintuitiveness disappears with time. I am unsure whether the view is true or false, but it is at least intellectually appealing, and on reflection it is not too crazy to be acceptable.[48]

Once understood, Kurt Gödel's (1906–78) 1931 paper, "On formally undecidable propositions of Principia Mathematica [by A. N. Whitehead (1861–1947) and Bertrand Russell (1872–1970)] and related systems," devastated a generation of mathematicians. The dream of ever-expanding applications of the axiomatic method was cast in doubt. Gödel proved that there would be propositions in an axiomatic system rich enough for the formulation of arithmetic the truth of which could not be decided by step-by-step deductions from those axioms. This had, and continues to have, dramatic consequences, as we have seen, for both AI and the human brain. The rules within complex computers seem to be governed by the range of possibilities circumscribed by the Gödel results. The human mind, however, seems not to be so circumscribed, as Penrose seeks to establish.

"Meaning is always a step away from anything you can observe in the world"

The linguist and philosopher Jan Koster writes:

> I think the Gödel results are the most important philosophical contribution of the twentieth century and I think I tend to generalize the spirit of his insights to all of meaning: just as it is impossible to completely formalize mathematics, it is impossible to reduce meaning to any form of scientific description. Meaning is always a step away from anything you can observe in the world. What you can find in the neural machinery of the brain is not meaning but codes. All codes, no matter how intricately structured, are dead and only become alive through the interpretation (from "within") of the living subject. This "last step" kind of interpretation cannot be formalized without infinite regress. I think this idea is related to Gödel's and also behind Wittgenstein's remark that the interpretation of a representation is not a kind of shadow representation (Blue Book) [dictated to W's classes 1933–34, but only formally published in 1958]. One reason, by the way, I find brain studies disappointing in the long run is the "external" perspective: it tells you just as little about the mind as dissecting your computer would tell you about computation. The step from a complex structure of matter (like in the brain) to the rich internal world of meaning cannot be understood from the scientific, "external" point of view.[49]

Mind–body dualism vs materialism has been with us in some form since the Greeks. This should suggest to us that we are dealing with an ideological issue. What is pressing the issue to the fore once again? One contributor has been the computer-driven computability model of mind. Thirty-plus years ago, as computers began to exhibit real speed in computations, one found talk about programs in terms of "cells," "neural nets," etc. Although those who were then developing high-powered programs were mathematicians keenly sensitive to the Gödel–Turing results, the temptation on the part of some psychologists was to see in computers the possibility of developing an electronic representation of mind. In a 1958 *New Yorker Magazine* cartoon by Richter, two scientists are reading the tape just produced by a huge computer. One scientist says: "I'll be damned. It says, 'Cogito, ergo sum.'"

The psychologists knew that the computer model was a failure but they hoped that at least "in principle" all mental phenomena could be replicated by means of ever more elaborate computer programs installed in ever more complex electronic hardware. Of course computer innards do not look like the interior of a brain, as Koster notes. Nevertheless, certain mental activities can be simulated. Chess has always been an attractive test field because of the specificity attached to the rules governing the moves of the pieces and the constraints imposed by the board itself. It takes incredible ingenuity to develop a computer programmed to play chess at grand-master level but it is still not the equivalent of human activity, nor is there any basis for thinking that this constitutes an explanation of how the human mind/brain works. As Descartes remarked, humans can talk about anything they choose and they can respond "appropriately" (or not) to what is said to them. Like "teaching" chimpanzees to replicate various human activities (e.g. speech), the computational model of mind seems to have been put aside, although it gets a new lease on life every time a new and more powerful computer chip is designed or a new "miniaturization" step is taken. These steps are important and exciting and will undoubtedly contribute to the remarkable new developments which continue to arise in several sciences, e.g. in physics, genetics, medicine, etc. Computers have played a decisive role in virtually all major scientific work over the last score of years. What computers will not do is provide us with what Searle calls "an adequate science of the brain," except in the familiar but vacuous "in principle" sense.

The work of biologists, physicists, linguists, radiologists, and neurologists, soon began to be pooled and new techniques for the study of the brain became possible. The most exciting results were the imaging studies made possible by PET (positron emission tomography) and MRI (magnetic resonance imaging) scans. Earlier studies of the brain of necessity had to rely on such things as brain damaged patients (injured war veterans were a boon to research) and to try to map the roles of different parts of the brain in conjunction with certain sorts of behavior deficits. Thus imaging studies seemed to promise a "great leap forward" for the study of the brain. Lovely multi-colored pictures could be produced showing what was happening when, for example, a human subject utters or hears various linguistic expressions. That one can video the brain while it engages in, say, some linguistic activity seems to be exciting for some scientists. One is, so to speak, peering inside the "language faculty." Given that syntacticians are just beginning to get a handle on the linguistic side of things, it is hard to understand what neuroscientists think they can discover other than to confirm what we have known for at least a century, i.e. the seat of the language faculty is in a certain part of the brain! On the other hand, this sort of research is encouraged because it requires marvelous machines and it seems to attract vast amounts of research funds, and so less is available for work on the nitty-gritty of research in linguistics even though linguistics is one of the few disciplines which gives us a handle on the structure of the mind/brain, albeit without the benefit of pretty pictures.

A footnote on funds dedicated to fads: it may be hard to believe now, but twenty-odd years ago, funds were lavishly dispensed to show that animals could learn language. This was important, because Descartes and Chomsky both claimed that language was a uniquely human possession. The innateness which Descartes and Chomsky held was essential to understanding the development of human speech ran headlong into behaviorist ideology. So it became a way to "refute" the Cartesian model of human nature in the interest of behaviorism. Behaviorism is still around but that particular "refutation" is now just an embarrassment.

Neuroscience runs into another problem. Neuroscientists have all along been trying to make sense of the tiny brains of slugs, etc., that is, animals whose brains are constituted by a very small number of cells. Given the billions of brain cells which we are said to possess, the difficulties posed by a brain with only a handful of cells (each of which is still only partially understood) suggests that extrapolation to the complexities of the human brain can only be by way of metaphorical fantasy.

I take the mind–body problem to be a mystery. I agree with Chomsky that Newton demolished the notion of *body* and hence made materialism incoherent. But neither Newton nor Chomsky seem to have successfully communicated that to the natives. And so I prefer to fall back on the notion of *mystery*. However, that is not what I find interesting. What I find interesting about the mind–body problem is that it constitutes an ideological litmus test. I take the dispute between empiricists and rationalists, with which the mind–body problem is connected, to be the deepest and most pervasive conflict within the Republic of Letters over at least the past four centuries, if not since the days of Greek philosophy. And scientists and philosophers have chosen sides in accordance with their views about the malleable, plastic human nature of the empiricists or the more autonomous and pre-structured human nature of the rationalists. Let us now explore some of the directions in which this dispute, which seems to stand at the very foundation of our entire culture, has been moving.

When books are burned, when authors are banned, when ideas are suppressed, it is a pretty good sign that something important is being said. Descartes seems to have been unpopular with a very large number of people. Yves-Marie André SJ, Malebranche's biographer, did prison time in the Bastille for his Cartesian views. All of this is surprising, given that philosophers may not seem likely candidates for being Public Enemies. Special cases do arise. The Catholic doctrine of transubstantiation says that in the miracle of the mass, the bread and wine, when consecrated, retain the same "accidents" which they had at the outset. That is, their sensible qualities (color, taste, etc.) remain the same. What changes is said to be the *substance* in which these qualities inhere, that is, the body and blood of Christ. The framework within which the doctrine is expressed has a very specific account of accidents, qualities, and substances. If one alters the framework, one runs the risk that the doctrine can no longer be coherently expressed. Not all Catholics accepted the (Aristotelian) framework which seemed to be required to make sense of the doctrine (first formally articulated at the Council of Trent [1545–63]). This obviously created problems for those who wished to remain orthodox Catholics but who rejected the Aristotelian-style framework. There were very extended theological debates over the metaphysics of the change, specifically how one substance could shift to being another. For example, was there an instantaneous blending of the two substances prior to the change or was one substance totally annihilated and then instantaneously replaced by another? Both seemed to require that the qualities be able to subsist independently through the change – something qualities, being entities which *must* inhere in a substance, cannot ordinarily do.

One can easily recognize the difficulties which resistance to accepting a certain framework can generate when one turns back to the medieval period and explores the puzzles which expressing transubstantiation within different schemes can cause. And there are echoes of these matters when one turns to such topics as the status of women, or when human conception takes place. But Descartes seems to have offended and disturbed all sorts of people and he is still doing it! What went wrong? There are not only the arguments of the anti-foundationalists just discussed. These are not attacks on filigree details of Descartes's writings. There are literally thousands of criticisms aiming to show, for example, that by means of highly sophisticated logical techniques one can discern errors, often minute, in Descartes's procedures. Ryle, Rorty, Taylor, and legions of anti-foundationalists direct frontal attacks which challenge the very core of Descartes's position. Still, although those discussions are largely of interest only to the academic community one is entitled to ask why so many have a stake in his refutation, and just what that stake is.

Three hundred years after Descartes's *Meditations* was published, Ryle feels compelled to claim that a misuse of language infected Descartes's talk about minds and bodies, and thereby to "refute" Descartes's central argument. Surely there is something strange about feeling compelled to see Descartes as a continuing menace after three hundred years of refutations and challenges. The same holds for the anti-foundationalists who contributed to *After Philosophy: end or transformation?* It is hard to think of another thinker who has had such a bad press for so long and who has been the object of such vituperative criticism. Occasionally a philosopher is denounced and becomes an object of scorn for a limited period. Karl Popper, for example, wrote a violent attack on Plato (and Hegel), *The Open Society and its Enemies* (1945), arguing that various ideas in Plato had been root causes of both left- and right-wing totalitarianism. Popper's arguments generated considerable discussion at the time, but Plato survived that brief encounter largely unscathed. Descartes did not have such good fortune!

More than three and a half centuries have now passed since Descartes wrote. He led no army; he founded no school; he held no university post; he headed no political movement; he sought no political office; his philosophical reputation really rests on a very few books; he apparently tried to avoid giving offence to his fellow Catholics, or, for that matter, to Protestants of his acquaintance. Some commentators have said that Descartes is really an atheist, or an unbeliever, but I think it is presumptuous to say that one has a litmus test for certifying a person's religious beliefs in the face of their claims to be believers. In any case, there are apparently lots of philosophers and theologians of the seventeenth and eighteenth centuries who are accused of being heterodox. Why pick on Descartes?

Somehow a popular, influential, and learned twentieth-century Pope can write a book in which, among other things, Descartes's views are taken as a major threat to both Christianity and to European culture. This is an altogether remarkable event, and so is the fact that the print run is said to be five million copies. How has Descartes emerged as the philosopher philosophers love to hate, and why has the debate been moved from the halls of the learned to a worldwide context? This is of a totally different order from the complaints of the philosophers. Millions of people listen when the Pope speaks. Why has the Pope attacked him? Perhaps it is true that the pen is mightier than the sword!

In his 1994 book, *Crossing the Threshold of Hope*,[50] Pope John Paul II (1920–), himself well schooled in philosophy, discusses a range of difficulties concerning God. A popular press article has even appeared headlined: "Why the Pope blames Descartes for God's death."[51] The Pope writes:

> It seems to me that [the questions you ask] stem from another source, *one that is purely rationalist, one that is characteristic of modern philosophy* – the history of which begins with Descartes, who split thought from existence and identified existence with reason itself: "*Cogito, ergo sum*". (p. 38)

> [Descartes] *distanced us from the philosophy of existence*, and also from the traditional approaches of Saint Thomas which lead us to God who is "autonomous existence" … By making subjective consciousness absolute, Descartes moves instead toward *pure consciousness of the Absolute*, which is *pure thought* … Only that which corresponds to human thought makes sense. The objective truth of this thought is not as important as the fact that something exists in human consciousness … (p. 51) Though the father of modern rationalism certainly cannot be blamed for the move away from Christianity, it is difficult not to acknowledge that he created the climate in which, in the modern era, such an estrangement became possible. (p. 52)

Thus John Paul believes that the ultimate root causes of the sins of modernity and the corruption generated by the Enlightenment are the writings of Descartes. The Pope is not alone, of course, in attributing the decline and fall of practically everything to Descartes. It is Descartes who is charged with setting off three and a half centuries of separating thought from the world, thought which should be seen as being generated by the objective world and not being taken to be the world of objectivity in itself. It is downhill from Descartes to Marx and liberalism, from the seventeenth-century scientific revolution to the French and Russian revolutions.

John Paul offers his diagnosis of what has "gone wrong" in our culture, how Descartes's separation of thought and existence has corrupted our worldviews. He hopes to make us see the importance of defeating rationalism and returning to the values of the medieval world and to the empiricist thesis that "there is nothing in the intellect that is not first in the senses" (p. 33). Only in that way can we hope to wage a successful war against both rationalism and the Enlightenment.

The Pope is not the only one to fear the consequences of the Enlightenment. Environmentalists often take a very dim view of the "mechanization of the world picture" to which Descartes made such a signal contribution. They often demonize Descartes for what appears to them to be a lack of sensitivity towards animals and the rest of the natural world. Although as noted above, Descartes's opinion is nuanced, he is inclined to consider animals as machines and probably without souls. He believed that humans had intellectual/cognitive capacities which were different in kind from those exhibited by animals. Humans show their mental abilities through language. Animals, however skillful in other matters, lack language except in some metaphorical sense. This was hardly a new claim. Moreover, the Christian tradition generally holds that Christ died to redeem humans, not animals.

There was no shortage among the ancient philosophers who attributed souls to animals. Aristotle, for whom souls were principles of development, motion, and life, had various levels of souls throughout the biological world. Still, humans possessed a rational soul different in kind from a (mere) animal soul. Thomas Aquinas subscribed to a similar version except that he wanted to be sure that the human soul had an "operation" in which the body does not share.[52] In his sixteenth-century *Apology for Raimond Sebond*, Montaigne regales us with stories and tales, culled from classical literature, about animals, their moral capacity, their sense of obligation, their faithfulness, their intellectual achievements, etc. Some indication of the huge extent of the seventeenth-century literature on the question of the "souls of beasts" can be found in Pierre Bayle's *Dictionary* articles *Rorarius* and *Pereira*. Leibniz argued that the version of dualism which emerged within his own theory of monads made possible a less confrontational picture, so to speak, of animal souls. Bayle was not convinced. The matter of animal souls became, in the late seventeenth century, a device for attacking dualism of the sort advanced by Descartes and Malebranche.

In addition to fear that the mechanization of the world picture yields attitudes of contempt towards Earth, environmentalists also fear that the ideology of the Enlightenment both strengthens and supplements biblical attitudes not religiously but because of the enhancement of human technological power and the dream of unending progress which it generates. That is, the thesis that God has given us the earth and the animals which inhabit it and hence that our exploitation of these gifts is virtually an obligation.

Perhaps Descartes's own attempt to reject empiricism and establish *rationalist foundations* for knowledge fails, but it is important to see why he chose innate ideas and why innate ideas were taken by his opponents to be such an offense. Innate ideas already play a part in Plato's theory of knowledge. In the dialogue, *Meno*, Plato's spokesman Socrates elicits from a slave boy a variety of geometrical truths which the boy had never been taught. Plato believes that the boy "recollected" these truths from a prior life. So innateness in some form is hardly a new doctrine. And it was not unheard of among the medievals or, as noted above, Aquinas would not have felt compelled to refute it.

The case of John Calvin, another defender of innate ideas, illuminates the reason the doctrine generated offense. Calvin wanted the idea of God to be innate. He did not want anything to intervene between our consciousness and God. To be concrete, he did not want the Roman Church, the Pope, the bishops, or the priests to interfere with the possibility of our direct access to God. The Church, on the other hand, held that *it* was the vehicle that enabled us to reach God. That is why the Church has always held that in virtue of Christ's words to Peter, "upon this rock I will build my church ..." (Matthew 16:18) it possesses the "keys to the kingdom [of God]" and thus that there is no salvation outside the Church.

The Cartesian theory of knowledge in effect removes the privileged role of the Church (and all other authorities). Each person has a foundation within his or her own mind which provides a basis for us to understand God and to discover truths in virtue of which we may be saved. A minority within the Church had always emphasized the privacy of human conscience and had minimized the control of the mind, but the majority position within the Church, and within the many political organizations affiliated with it, was always dedicated to preserving and expanding its power. Simply put, Descartes's foundationalism was perceived to be a threat to good order.

Seventeenth-century authorities soon discovered that the new account of human nature, the dualist account, had an awkward consequence. People would automatically be seen to have a measure of "mental" privacy. Yet it was crucially important that governments have access to what people were "thinking" about. That had always been a problem, but behavior was traditionally seen as providing an adequate window into the minds of the natives. The older ideology did not give minds a privileged position. If I am correct about Cartesian dualism, the perceived threat caused by this new doctrine was that it placed an ontological barrier between the individual and the authoritarian Church or state. This hardly pleased kings, bishops, or pastors. To remedy the situation, governments turned to oaths. By means of oaths it was hoped that it would be possible to "squeeze" the truth out of recalcitrant minds because oaths called upon God to enforce a link between the oath-taker's words and the oath-taker's thoughts and thereby to "externalize" minds and make them subject to control. By invoking God in this process, by insisting on the importance of truth-telling before God, the ensuing threat of eternal damnation was intended to guarantee that oaths would do their work and conspiracies against the king would be detected. The appeal to oaths required care and caution. Calvinists and other Protestants were defenders of the rights of conscience and imposing oaths would appear to undermine that core doctrine, a doctrine they had erected against the papists. But resistance weakened. Thus Archbishop Tillotson (1630–94) said:

> The Necessity of Religion to the support of human Society, in nothing appears more evidently than in this, The Obligation of an Oath, which is so necessary for the Maintenance of Peace and Justice among Men, depends wholly upon the Sense and Belief of a Deity.

> For no reason can be imagined why any Man that doth not believe a
> God, should make the least conscience of an Oath, which is nothing
> else but a solemn appeal to God as a Witness of the Truth of what we
> say.[53]

Bishop William Fleetwood (1656–1723) said similar things: "An Oath," he maintains, "is a most Religious thing; 'tis an acknowledgement of God's Omniscience ... [and] that we believe he knows the very Secrets of our Hearts." He adds that by an Oath, "I call God to witness that my Heart and Mouth agree."[54] Sometimes, quite contrary to the dualist ideology to which governments at least initially subscribed, a behavioral test was added to the oath. Thus in Britain, office holders were expected to be seen taking Holy Communion on a regular basis. It was assumed that secret Catholics would not dare to take Communion in the Church of England. John Locke is famous as an early defender of religious toleration, but he trusted neither Catholics nor their oaths. Atheists were beyond the pale. Lacking a belief in God, there was no fire and brimstone "enforcement procedure" for atheists or for Catholics. The difficulty with Catholics was that their oaths might be annulled by a Pope.

"There never was a civilized nation of any other complexion than white"

In this final chapter five domains with intellectual roots in Cartesian foundationalism are discussed: first, George Orwell's attempt to escape the grasp of totalitarian forces by means of a Cartesian-like step; second, a rationalist education policy and the negative impact of postmodernism upon it; third, racist theory and doctrines of human nature; fourth, sexism and dualism; and fifth, Cartesian dualism as a basis for freedom-of-speech absolutism.

1. A modern and powerful expression of a radically foundationalist position is to be found in George Orwell's *Nineteen Eighty-four*. Where Descartes's position emerges within the context of his attempt to find a basis for truth which is not subject either to doubt or to demonic forces or in any way dependent on authorities, Orwell (1903–50) is primarily troubled by the demonic forces available to an all-powerful state. This is how Orwell's character Winston considers the matter in chapter seven:

> In the end the Party would announce that two and two made five, and you would have to believe it. It was inevitable that they should make that claim sooner or later: the logic of their position demanded it … With the feeling … that he was setting forth an important axiom, he wrote: *Freedom is the freedom to say that two plus two make four. If that is granted, all else follows.* (Orwell's emphasis)

Orwell thought we should make no mistake about the lust for power which permeates political and community organizations. He believed that all such organizations insist upon getting "inside" our minds so as to be able to exercise complete control over us. To fail in that quest is to fail politically. He took his foundationalist appeal to basic arithmetical truths to be the only buckler against tyranny available to us.

2. Eighteenth-century Scotland witnessed considerable concern over education. What the Scots seem to have worried about was how to "educate for democracy." That has never proved to be an easy task. However, their educational system started out more democratic and less elitist than its English counterpart – presumably because of the different religious traditions which had taken hold in Scotland at the time of the Protestant Reformation. But the Scots were apprehensive about the English-style education model which was affecting their own. The English model was empiricist in flavor and aimed to produce highly qualified specialists. And the English certainly produced generations of classical scholars to be shipped off to staff the bureaucracies of the colonies. That, however, is not what the Scots wanted. They wanted an educational system that would cultivate our natures. Given that they generally subscribed to a rationalist picture of human nature, they rejected the claim that the human mind begins life as a blank tablet. Instead, they believed there was a core of reason within each human that they hoped a good education would enrich and enhance – but not create.[55]

The Scottish philosophy of common sense flourished for the better part of two centuries. The Scots believed that philosophy, and what they took to be closely related disciplines, should stand at the very center of the educational process for *all* students. They believed that a democratic society requires that its citizens study some of the general problems and concerns that we face simply by virtue of being human and as being members of a society. Philosophy (in a broad sense) was thus assigned the task of cultivating those features of the human intellect that we hold in common. And here is the point: they held that democracy requires that everyone have an educated sense for individual, social, and political matters. Lacking such a universally educated sense we become ready targets for tyranny. Thus from Descartes, through Bayle and the Scots, to Orwell we see a constant worry about our sensitivity to tyrannical forces, and about our having an innate capacity to think independently. On the other hand, for those who seek power to control our minds and bodies, it is easy to appreciate why Descartes and the traditions he spawned are irritating obstructions.

Descartes did not think that he lived at a time and place where he could depend on the existence of a community of scholars whose members were open to ideas and free to explore unpopular views in accordance with an ideal of the sort Bayle, and to a lesser extent, the Scots, hoped for. Descartes was in fact genuinely terrified by the Inquisition's condemnation of Galileo. Apprehensive lest a similar fate might befall him since, like Galileo, he accepted the heliocentric hypothesis, Descartes withheld from publication some early work, *The World* and his *Treatise on Man*. These were apparently parts of a single work, written in French during 1629–33, which were only published posthumously. His *Rules for the Direction of the Mind*, written in Latin in about 1628, was not published until a Dutch translation appeared in 1684. It lacks the philosophical subtlety and many of the distinctions which taking scepticism seriously obliged Descartes to make in the *Discourse* and the *Meditations,* but it does reflect his dedication to method. Although Descartes seems often to have generated unnecessary conflicts within the Dutch community, he sought to minimize his troubles once he appreciated that an opponent had political power and influence. He hoped, but to no avail, that by dedicating the *Meditations* to the Faculty of Theology at the Sorbonne, his work might be accepted and taught in the schools. He was proved wrong. Clerical criticisms and condemnations soon came his way and not long after his death his writings, as noted above, went on the *Index of Prohibited Books*. Nevertheless, Descartes was soon taught in Protestant institutions both inside and outside of The Netherlands, specifically in Saumur and Geneva,[56] but not without frequent struggles. Aristotle often retained his hold on universities until at least the mid-nineteenth century.

John Locke, himself an anti-Cartesian, saw what was at stake in controversies over human nature. He held that the mind sets out in the world as a "blank tablet." For those charged with setting out educational policy it has proven to be a useful and powerful metaphor. It not only suggests that we are empty, malleable organisms, but it also suggests that we are available for those who would like to "write," as it were, on our blank tablets. Locke also rejects the notion of a fixed human nature, since the human mind is totally flexible. There is a scale from the low end of our species up to the level of angels, and it is a scale without gaps. Thus neither species nor genus are fixed. Locke writes: "I once saw a Creature that was the Issue of a Cat and a Rat" (*Essay*, III, vi, § 23).

Descartes and Orwell fear the manipulative power of churches, states, or parties, and all those who claim or seek to possess authority over our thought processes. All such authority is taken to be illegitimate. Locke is on the other side. He was politically a very powerful person in his own right. And he wrote for the winning side. Where Descartes sought to develop his foundationalist position and to erect a block to control, Locke might be thought of as one of the first explicit anti-foundationalists. A doctrine of human nature built on empiricist grounds aims to facilitate control and to convince us that we are plastic and malleable while at the same time creating a place for those whose claim to power rests on nothing more than their attributing to themselves an expertise in the matter of "writing" on our blank tablets. Where those in power once claimed they had a warrant from God to control our access to heaven, now we find certain social scientists appealing to their scientific "knowledge" as justifying their own accession to political power and hence their "right" to control our fate. Given the track-record of, say, economists in predicting how humans will behave in the market place, or how to keep unemployment in what they take to be a proper balance, it may seem remarkable that the credentials which give them access to power are so seldom seriously challenged. But their credentials are embedded in the empiricist ideology, and we have seen that great efforts have been expended over three and a half centuries to eliminate the threat to that ideology posed by Descartes and rationalism.

Closely related to matters of educational policy, the so-called postmodernists have moved to eliminate the foundationalist option by effectively dissolving all standards in ethics, in legal theory, as well as in science – and even in logic and mathematics. They eliminate any basis in human nature for any standards in those domains, standards which have traditionally been sustained by rationalism. In carrying out the wholesale elimination of standards, the postmodernists are hoist on their own petard insofar as they employ putative arguments to "establish" their cases. Having dissolved logic, it is hard to see how they are entitled to advance arguments. But by treating us as "foundationless" beings, they deprive us of any standpoint from which we can battle tyranny. The rejoinder of the postmodernists to complaints either about their acceptance of traditional relativism or their dissolution of logic and argument is to argue (!) that they make no claims to truth, that they only note the uses of power in the service of ideologies. In fact, they advance a variant of the argument of Thrasymachus which so troubled Plato in the *Republic*, that might makes right. Who are the postmodernists? In varying ways Rorty and Taylor may be included. But the movement can be said to begin with Nietzsche (1844–1900), Heidegger (1889–1976), and Paul de Man (1919–83), and continued by Foucault (1926–84) and Jacques Derrida (1930–). It is not an easily defined movement or tendency but it can be characterized negatively: it is against Cartesian foundationalism.

Whenever and wherever rationalism appears, every effort is made to attack it. The most important modern instance has been in the work of the behaviorists. At mid-twentieth century behaviorism sought to establish itself as the most "scientific" methodology for psychology. It provided a methodology which entailed that there was no reason to introduce "mind" into science. The animal kingdom (including humans) was populated by entities whose "knowledge" was entirely a matter of external input. This "empty organism" thesis was quickly accepted by those scientists exploring language acquisition. Perhaps more important, it provided a "scientific" core for all of the so-called social sciences, from psychology to sociology to political science to education. It proved to be an attractive model for ideological reasons. It meant that the "teachers" were in a position to control the contents of "minds." It also meant that those who were in a position to "control" content, whether in universities, the government, or the media, had very real stakes in the preservation of this methodology. Indeed, their political power depended in large part on their skill in convincing people that those very same people were in fact as plastic as the model suggests.[57] That is why the dispute between empiricists and rationalists has been of transcendent importance from the time of Plato and Aristotle to the present. That is also why attempts to "solve" the mind–body problem or dissolve the ensuing basic tensions between empiricism and rationalism are likely to fail. The important question is how these ideologies are used – and to what ends.

3. Racism is another area in which one can explore the importance of the empiricist model. It is said that before the last part of the seventeenth century racism had not yet emerged on the Western cultural scene. Obviously all sorts of linguistic, ethnic, and religious differences had been noted among humankind. So had differences in color. People had found ample reasons to fight, disparage, and kill one another. But these differences did not challenge the idea that humans were all one species. Humans were *essentially* one and the variations were, in the philosophically technical sense, *accidental*. Léon Poliakov writes that François Bernier (1620–88) sorted out "four or five" different "species or races" of men. He considered the blackness of the African essential whereas the darkness of the Hindu was accidental. Leibniz reportedly criticized Bernier for suggesting that all humans are not of the same race. Poliakov writes that Bernier's classification is "perhaps the first writing in which the term 'race' appears in its modern sense."[58]

Most myths of origin, prior to Bernier, operated within a biblical context. Employing biblical anthropology, and constrained by the time limits creationism required,[59] the task was to find loose ends, so to speak, in the Bible stories which could provide a hook on which to locate various newly discovered tribes and cultures. This became especially difficult with the discovery of the so-called New World. There was a very extended debate over the status of South American Indians. It was settled by Pope Paul III's *Sublimus Deus* (1537). The concern was not racial; the concern was whether the Indians were properly human and hence whether they could be converted to Catholicism. They were. Later, from the seventeenth to the early nineteenth centuries, the indigenous North American peoples were often thought to be members of the lost tribes of Israel. As Jews, their conversion to Christianity was especially dear in God's eyes.

Bernier was a follower of Gassendi and an acquaintance of John Locke. And it is in Locke that we find various philosophical claims that provide a framework within which racist doctrine could be formulated. Locke breaks with the tradition which holds that substances have essential properties. He lets us continue to use the language of essence and accident, but we decide what should count as essential. We find a cluster of properties and choose to call them essential. To take one of Locke's favorite examples, gold is yellow, malleable, heavy, soluble in aqua regia, etc. But there is no "glue" in the world linking what Locke calls a substance with the properties it exhibits. No link, in other words, between gold (taken as the substance) and yellow or malleable or heavy (the properties). There are no physical links among the various properties which might explain why these particular properties happen to be grouped together in one substance. They just happen to be together, largely because of the selection we have made on the basis of our own preferences. Nor are there any logical links, of the sort we might find in geometrical figures, which bind these properties together. Locke interpreted philosophers, presumably such as Descartes and Malebranche, of speaking (in effect) of a metaphysical "glue" which would bind various properties together so that necessary connections on the analogue of geometry could be found. But Locke finds no necessary connections of the sort he apparently thinks others have discovered. He bewails the fact that he has not discerned, for example, any "necessary connection between malleableness and the color or weight of gold" (*Essay*, IV, vi, § 10). Since we are ignorant of the *real* essences of things, we are obliged to deal only with what he describes as the *nominal* essences of things, and these essences are entirely of our own construction. These are all accidental rather than essential. Two things follow: (1) "human" becomes a flexible category depending on what properties we *choose* to include. (2) We are now free to let properties which had been thought purely accidental, like human skin color, count as essential. Thus is provided a basis for the ready formulation of a racist position.

Locke writes:

> A Child having fram'd the *Idea* of a *Man*, it is probable, that his *Idea* is just like that Picture, which the Painter makes of the visible Appearances joyn'd together; and such a Complication of *Ideas* together in his Understanding, makes up the single complex *Idea* which he calls *Man*, whereof White or Flesh colour [!!] in *England* being one, the Child can demonstrate to you, that *a Negro is not a Man*, because White-colour was one of the constant simple *Ideas* of the complex *Idea* he calls *Man: And therefore he can demonstrate by the Principle, It is impossible for the same Thing to be, and not to be ...* that a *Negro is not a Man* (*Essay*, IV, vii, § 16)

If Locke would reject the child's view, he could not do it in any principled way. He gives us no guidelines for deciding whether a negro is a man or whether the progeny of [man]drills[60] and women (cf. *Essay,* III, vi, § 23) are human beyond the similar sorts of decisions we make about, say, gold.

I have not claimed that Locke was a racist. However, Locke was a defender of (perpetual) slavery. He compiled the *Fundamental Constitutions of Carolina.* Section CX provides that every freeman "shall have absolute power and authority over his negro slaves." What is important about Locke in these connections is that he breaks so radically with the rationalist model and opts instead for the empiricist one. He is a fierce opponent of innate ideas. Indeed, he devotes the entire first book of his *Essay* to refuting all versions of the theory of innate ideas that he can think of! He maintains that our minds are initially *blank tablets.* His anti-rationalism, his anti-dualism, also appears from the fact that he was something of a materialist and that he allowed that the atomic structure might be such that matter might think. In brief, he took every opportunity to dismember the rationalist account of human nature.

Another name in the pantheon of empiricist philosophers is David Hume (1711–76). Where Locke seems to have provided a framework which facilitated the expression of racist theories, David Hume was in a position to utilize that framework:

> I am apt to suspect the negroes, and in general all the other species of men (for there are four or five different kinds) to be naturally

inferior to the whites. There never was a civilized nation of any other complexion than white, nor even any individual eminent either in action or speculation. No ingenious manufactures amongst them, no arts, no sciences. On the other hand, the most rude and barbarous of the whites, such as the ancient GERMANS, the present TARTARS, have still something eminent about them, in their valour, form of government, or some other particular. Such a uniform and constant difference could not happen, in so many countries and ages, if nature had not made an original distinction betwixt these breeds of men. Not to mention our colonies, there are NEGROE slaves dispersed all over EUROPE, of which none ever discovered any symptoms of ingenuity; tho' low people, without education, will start up amongst us, and distinguish themselves in every profession. In JAMAICA indeed they talk of one negro as a man of parts and learning; but 'tis likely he is admired for very slender accomplishments, like a parrot, who speaks a few words plainly.[61]

There is a considerable literature in the eighteenth century on the question of racism raised by Hume. One of Hume's most vociferous critics was James Beattie (1735–1803).[62] He argued from a dualist standpoint. So did his fellow Scot, James Ramsay (1733–89), a student of Thomas Reid (1710–96). Ramsay criticized Hume for denying that "the soul is a simple substance, not to be distinguished by squat or tall, black, brown, or fair."[63] Ramsay is thus criticizing Hume's color/intelligence correlation, a correlation which he takes to be an absurd consequence of Hume's empiricism. In fact, he considers the entire correlation game to be a mistake. Instead, he appeals directly to the Cartesian notion that the soul is a simple substance to which colors do not apply. Thus both Beattie and Ramsay interpret Hume's philosophy as facilitating his racism and they both take versions of rationalism to provide protection against racism.

Travelers' reports poured into Europe from the fifteenth century onward. They made it difficult to retain the biblical story of human origins. The more generous commentators could hold that the "inferiority" of blacks and others was not God-given. It was a product of their having degenerated. But the degeneration was not the mark of essential differences. The degenerative states could be remedied by good food, good living, and good education. But the majority view, held by people like Hume and Thomas Jefferson, saw specific differences where people like the abbé Henri Grégoire (1750–1831) saw remediable weaknesses.[64]

Philosophers have tended not to notice Hume's remarks on blacks nor, for that matter, the fact that Immanuel Kant (1724–1804) cited them. And they have tended to ignore both Beattie's comments and those of Ramsay. It is especially puzzling that Grégoire's study, *De la littérature des negres*[65] (quickly translated into English), was ignored. It was a detailed refutation of Hume-type remarks. Grégoire's refutation was constructed by finding all sorts of blacks who, contrary to Hume, were preeminent in one domain or another. Gradually, of course, polygenetic theories began to appear although such theories ran counter to the Bible. For example, one heretical theory, very influential in the nineteenth century, held that there were men before Adam (the Pre-Adamite theory) and hence multiple creations.[66]

To convert Cartesian dualism into a framework suitable for articulating racism, it would be crucially helpful to be able to show how colors could apply to *minds*. But the sharp dualist position and the claim that the human essence is mind or thought make this task very difficult. Given human ingenuity, perhaps it could have been done – but there was no need. The Lockian model was available. And of course the propagandist "need" to defend slavery was very real.

4. Closely related to the matter of racism is sexism. First of all, just as color terms do not apply to Cartesian minds, so neither do gender terms. Gender variation bears on the body, not on the soul. After all, much of Descartes's argument is directed at establishing a "real distinction" between the soul and the body. Secondly, Descartes seems to have been interested in having women read and study his ideas. There is nothing patronizing in his remarks to Princess Elisabeth although she is a score of years younger than he is. Gaukroger writes:

> Cartesianism was in fact developed into a specific social philosophy at an early stage, and François Poulain de la Barre, in his *Discours physique de moral de l'égalité de deux sexes, où l'on voit l'importance de*

se défaire des préjugez (1673), applied the "method of doubt" and the doctrine of clear and distinct ideas to the prejudices of the day, and unmasked the falsity of one of the greatest of these prejudices, the inequality of women, offering one of the first and most articulate defences of feminism in the early modern era. Indeed, there was a group of women thinkers – which included Descartes' niece, Catherine – who in the 1670s developed a version of Cartesian philosophy in which Cartesianism was proposed as an alternative (with women particularly in mind) to the philosophies of the schools and Académie.[67]

There has, of course, been a modern debate about whether the separation of minds and bodies can be drawn in ways which support feminism. I simply note that the argument has been advanced that it can.

5. Not long after Descartes's death, philosopher/theologians began to notice that a strong theory of conscience could be embedded in Cartesian dualism. The link was easy enough to make. On the one hand, appeals to the privacy of conscience seemed to have a direct connection with a defense of religious toleration. After all, there seemed to be no way to probe consciences. And so Calvinists who took positions which they then claimed to be matters of conscience seemed to have secured the high ground in debate since the "voice" of conscience was said to be the voice of God. But when the dispute turned on the correct interpretation of a passage of Scripture, especially when it concerned a principle which divided one religious group from another, commitment to conscience was often surrendered. On the one hand, some Calvinists defended what they called the "rights of an erring conscience." That is, a thesis might generally be taken to be objectively wrong but if held with a pure conscience then it must count, *for that person*, as true. On the other hand, some people felt that defenders of the truth, so to speak, since they too were entitled to appeal to the doctrine of the rights of the erring conscience, could apply persuasive force to those committed to an "erroneous" position. It was in this context that Bayle argued on behalf of free speech. Critics of the theory of the erring conscience pointed out that it seemed to follow from the doctrine that one could commit, say, murder – or torture people for

holding heretical opinions – and simply maintain that one had acted with a pure conscience. But that was a consequence to be avoided. It should not follow from the doctrine of the rights of an erring conscience that murderers and torturers were to be excused if they claimed to have murdered or tortured while acting from pure consciences.

This is where freedom of speech enters the discussion: Bayle held that the rights of the erring conscience extended only to *talking* about murder but not to actual murder; talk was one thing, action was another. Physical coercion as a vehicle for conversion was known, pejoratively, as "forcing consciences" and it was a common feature throughout the seventeenth century's wars of religion. French Catholics had applied draconian punishments, as Bayle knew at first hand, to the Huguenots, and he knew that Protestants once in power might also use coercion. After all, Calvin himself had authorized the death sentence against Servetus (*c*. 1510–53) in Geneva, for heresy. Both Catholics and Calvinists believed that the civil authorities had an obligation to enforce religious conformity lest the salvation of the people be put at risk. There was of course, another motivation. The line between church and state had not yet been accepted although both Bayle and Locke had, for different reasons, drawn it. Governments feared that instability would follow if they released their control over religious groups.

Descartes knew from his experience in The Netherlands that members of different religions could live together without killing one another. As already noted, Bayle argued that there was no logical link between religion and morality and hence that a (moral) society of atheists was perfectly imaginable. Locke opposed freedom of speech but he defended religious toleration (within sharp constraints). Locke held that the rationale for a civil society covered the need for people to live in peace in this world with security for their person and their goods but that rationale certainly did not include guaranteeing us a place in the world to come. The price for failing to tolerate various religions (Locke held that Catholics and atheists were not to be tolerated) was social disorder and worse. Like Bayle he was appalled by the bloodshed and destruction which the wars of religion had caused.

Reflections on the roles of conscience, and of the mental privacy within which it was embedded, thus moved the discussion to matters of freedom of speech. Given the Cartesian dualist framework, speech was placed on the side of the mind. One can say that roughly speaking, Bayle's Cartesian-based distinction between talking and doing caught the eyes of those Americans who drafted the Constitution of the United States at the end of the eighteenth century. The idea was that one could say what one wished, and that the force of legal sanctions extended only to actions, not words. This fitted nicely with the ideas of those Americans who wanted sovereignty to rest with the people. And if the people are sovereign, then their sovereignty would be annulled were any "higher" agency authorized to control their speech. In effect, that "higher" agency would then be the sovereign. The doctrine that "the people are sovereign" makes for good political rhetoric, but the powers that be, having been ordained by God (Romans: 13), have never been comfortable with the opinion that sovereignty resides with the people. And at no time is that discomfort clearer than when freedom of speech is at issue.

Freedom of speech has never really been a very widely accepted ideal even among Americans who pay lip-service to the idea. If one wishes to undercut it, one way that has proven effective is to reject the mind–body dualism from which in the first instance it developed. Since people have lost sight of the dualist roots of the doctrine (except for the very occasional US Supreme Court justice), it is an easy move to hold that talking is a form of action and accordingly that there is no fundamental distinction between talking and doing. If the state can restrain one's arm, it can – as Pierre Jurieu claimed in the seventeenth century – restrain one's tongue. And despite a few bumps along the way, that is how things seem to be working out even in the most democratic societies.

Descartes was genuinely fed up with the criticism he received. He wrote an interesting and insightful letter to his good friend Hector-Pierre Chanut (1601–62), a French diplomat serving in Sweden. It was Chanut who arranged for Descartes's fatal trip to Stockholm for the purpose of instructing Queen Christina in his philosophy.

A certain Father Bourdin thought he had good reason to accuse me of being a sceptic, because I refuted the sceptics; and a certain minister [Voetius] tried to argue that I was an atheist, without giving any reason other than the fact that I tried to prove the existence of God. So what would they say if I undertook to examine the right value of all the things we can desire or fear, the state of the soul after death, how far we ought to love life, and how we ought to live in order to have no reason to fear losing our life? It would be pointless for me to have only those opinions which agree as closely as possible with religion and which are as beneficial as possible for the state: for my critics would still try to convince people that I had opinions which are opposed to both. And so the best thing I can do henceforth is to abstain from writing books. (Letter to Chanut, 1 November 1646. CSMK III, 299–300; AT iv, 536–537)

Descartes was right. His influence may often have been bizarre. That his impact on his own century was remarkable should not surprise us. He had made major contributions to mathematics, physics, physiology, and philosophy. But his influence throughout the last three hundred and fifty years is something of a puzzle because so much of the commentary and discussion has been, as he feared, negative. His arguments are routinely "refuted" and his point of view constantly both rejected and ridiculed. No one, except perhaps for a few specialists, seems to care much about the philosophical positions of, say, Richard Burthogge (1638–1701), Ralph Cudworth (1617–88), or Arnold Geulincx (1624–69). Descartes, however, is not only a philosopher whose ideas have always generated general interest, but almost more than any other philosopher, he has proved to be a target of hate. I have cast this discussion of Descartes and his philosophy within the larger framework of the empiricist–rationalist theories of human nature in order to help illuminate why Descartes's opinions antagonize certain people. I have taken up a variety of topics within which Cartesianism can be seen as an irritant to those purveying the dominant ideology. Understandably, their skills in removing or alleviating the irritant have been honed over time.

Thus an examination of anti-foundationalism helps make the stakes clear. Anti-foundationalists believe that taking Descartes seriously means taking seriously the notion that humans have a core which is not constructed from data imposed upon us from the "outside." Indeed, they maintain that there is no core. We are totally plastic. This is not a scientific thesis, although in its behaviorist form it may be wrapped in scientific jargon. It is a set of ideas composed and defended because it has proven useful to those in positions of power. And it certainly helps make this set of ideas plausible if people can be led to think that it has some sort of objective foundation, e.g. a scientific base. Cartesianism has had the nasty habit throughout its long history of showing that the Emperor is not wearing New Clothes. And so Cartesianism must be attacked, refuted, and ridiculed lest its lessons be both understood and accepted, to the detriment of the prevailing ideology. It is not in the interest of those in power and those who seek power to let that happen. And thus far it has not. In order to defeat scepticism so as to provide a secure foundation for science, Descartes introduced a hyperbolical doubt – the demon deceiver. And a primary task he set himself in the *Meditations* was to exorcize that demon. Little could he have expected that instead he would emerge as our culture's preeminent demonic intellectual force.

Glossary

Corporeal: material, bodily.

Empiricism: the doctrine that human knowledge is immediately grounded in the data which we derive directly from sense experience.

Epistemology: that part of philosophy concerned with theories of knowledge. The term is often said to have been first used by Immanuel Kant (1724–1804) but explicit systematic concern with the theory of knowledge as a full sub-section of philosophy begins in the seventeenth century.

Essence: the defining element of a substance.

Exorcism: usually a religious process for removing "devils" and other evil spirits which are said to inhabit the psyches of people. The exorcist, the person who actually conducts a formal exorcism, is usually a specially trained priest.

Foundationalism: the thesis that there is a basis in a real and independent world, physical or mental, for our knowledge. Countered by anti-foundationalism.

Huguenot: a French Protestant who follows the teachings of John Calvin.

Ideas: the contents of human consciousness; sometimes anything from sense experience; sometimes concepts, e.g. the objects of purely mathematical consciousness; sometimes just equivalent to "thoughts."

Index of Prohibited Books (*Index Librorum Prohibitorum*): a listing of books banned by the Roman Church. Sometimes books were banned "subject to correction." The first formal banning seems to have occurred in the mid-thirteenth century, but the Index was first published in 1559. Books deemed heretical or likely to be dangerous to "faith and morals" were often, but not always, candidates for inclusion. Books on the Index were not to be read by the faithful, except with permission. Abolished in 1996.

Inquisition: an administrative organization within the Catholic Church, from the middle ages to the present, dedicated to rooting out and punishing heresies. Now the Congregation for the Doctrine of the Faith (1965).

Manichean: a Christian (heretical) sect which saw the entire world as caught up in a fierce conflict between the principles of good and evil. Often discussed in the context of the so-called problem of evil, i.e. how evil can exist in a world created by a good God.

Ontology: that branch of philosophy concerned with the study of being. The term itself is ancient but like epistemology, it is of relatively modern use, i.e. late seventeenth but mainly eighteenth centuries.

Rationalism: the doctrine that human knowledge is grounded in innate ideas, i.e. ideas that are part of the structure of the human intellect.

Scholasticism: the philosophy of the "schools," i.e. the mode of philosophy (and theology) taught throughout the middle ages in Western Christian universities. Generally taken to be based on Aristotelian philosophy.

Substance: a being which can exist independently of other things. For Descartes only God, soul, and body (matter) meet this standard, whereas an Aristotelian substance is typically a living biological entity, a tree for example, containing a principle of growth and development.

Theocracy: a form of state governed by a religious figure or group (hence theocratic).

Notes

1. Stephen Gaukroger, *Descartes: An Intellectual Biography*, p. 23. This is the definitive biography.

2. "Although officially forbidden, the Roman Catholic cult was tolerated in the Netherlands, and Descartes always lived in places where he could practice his religion without hindrance", William R. Shea, *The Magic of Numbers and Motion*, p. 165. Parts of Friesland are said to have been largely untouched by the Reformation and remain Catholic to this day.

3. Discussed by William R. Shea in his important study: *The Magic of Numbers and Motion*, p. 94. Shea cites the account given in Adrien Baillet's Vie de Monsieur Des-Cartes, vol. I, p. 103; ibid., p. 190.

4. For a delightful study, written with easy grace, see Simon Schama, *The Embarrassment of Riches: an Interpretation of Dutch Culture in the Golden Age*. (New York: Vintage Books, 1987).

5. Luciano Floridi, 'The diffusion of Sextus Empiricus's works in the Renaissance,' *Journal of the History of Ideas*, LVI, 1995, 63–85. A book by Floridi on the subject is expected soon.

6. *Outlines*, p. 71. For complete references, see note 8.

7. Jean La Placette offers the argument. See R. H. Popkin, *The History of Scepticism from Erasmus to Spinoza* (rev. ed. Berkeley/Los Angeles: University of California Press, 1979), p. 14.

8. Sextus is available in four bilingual volumes in the Loeb Classical Library series. See also the highly commended English translation of the *Outlines* by the distinguished philosopher and logician, Benson Mates (Oxford: University Press, 1996). For a collection of ancient sceptical texts, together with an illuminating but often polemical interpretive commentary, see Julia Annas and Jonathan Barnes, *The Modes of Scepticism* (Cambridge: University Press, 1985).

9. *Discourse*, Part IV (HR I, 101; AT vi, 32). On the sources of the *cogito*, see for example Léon Blanchet, *Les antécédents historiques du "je pense, donc je suis"* (Paris: Félix Alcan, 1920) and Gareth B. Matthews, *Thought's Ego in Augustine and Descartes* (Ithaca: Cornell University Press, 1992).

10. Noam Chomsky, *Cartesian Linguistics* (New York: Harper & Row, 1966), pp. 77–78.

11. For a detailed discussion, see James McGilvray, *Chomsky: Language, Mind, and Politics* (Cambridge: Polity Press, 1999).

12. Letter to Mersenne, December 1638. Quoted by William R. Shea, *The Magic of Numbers and Motion*, p. 293n. Shea cites vol. II, p. 464 in the standard complete edition, *Oeuvres de Descartes*, ed. Charles Adam and Paul Tannery (AT). Shea's book is an essential companion for the reader of Descartes.

13. *Entretien avec Burman*, AT v, 176, 16 April 1648.

14. O. K. Bouwsma, "On many occasions I have in sleep been deceived" (1957 Presidential Address before the American Philosophical Association). Reprinted in his *Philosophical Essays* (Lincoln: University of Nebraska Press, 1965).

15. *The Philosophical Writings of Descartes* (Cambridge: UP, 1991), transl. John Cottingham, Robert Stoothoff, Dugald Murdoch, and Anthony Kenny (hereafter CSMK), Vol. III, p. 25.

16. Exodus 22:18, "Thou shalt not suffer a witch to live" (King James Version). Translated as *Sorceress* in the *Soncino Chumash*.

17. Quoted in Aldous Huxley, *The Devils of Loudon* (New York: Harper Torchbooks, 1952), p. 152.

18. In one of his last works, *Notes Directed against a Certain Programme*, a response to remarks by onetime friend, Regius of Utrecht, Descartes writes that color, etc., sensations are innate not in the sense of being like mathematical concepts, the building-blocks of knowledge, but rather only mental capacities which do not "resemble" features of the material world.

19. See Theo Verbeek, *Descartes and the Dutch: Early Reactions to Cartesian Philosophy, 1637–1650* (Carbondale, Ill.: Southern Illinois University Press, 1992). In what seems to have been customary for Descartes, he accused Regius (in his *Foundations of Physics*) of plagiarism. See Descartes's Preface to his *Principles of Philosophy*. Verbeek discusses this at p. 58.

20. Descartes is not impressed by the traditional arguments. See his letter to Hyperaspistes, August 1641 (CSMK III, 188 f; AT iii, 422 f). Hobbes raises the example (Third Set of Objections, objection 5, HR II, 67; AT vii, 180). Descartes didn't rise to his bait. But perhaps most significant, when Gassendi took up the point in commenting on *Meditation* III, his § 3, Descartes replied: "How do you know that one born blind has no idea of color, when often enough in our case even when the eyes are closed the sense of light and colour is stimulated?" (HR II, 215; AT vii, 363 20).

21. The metaphor is ancient. Cf. Aristotle, *De anima*, III, ch. 4, 430a.

22. Aquinas, *Summa Theologica*, Q. LXXV, art. 1.

23. P. F. Strawson, *Individuals* (London: Methuen, 1959), p. 116.

24. Descartes's *Passions of the Soul*, written in French in 1649. It was apparently the last work published by Descartes.

25. John Cottingham reports a grand total of 504 "articles." See his Translator's Preface to the *Principles* in the three-volume translation, *The Philosophical Writings of Descartes*, John Cottingham, Robert Stoothoff, Dugald Murdoch and Anthony Kenny. (Cambridge: UP, 1985 f); hereafter CSMK. See vol. I, p. 177.

26. See Theo Verbeek, *Descartes and the Dutch*. See also his major study, *René Descartes et Martin Schoock: La querelle d'Utrecht* (ed. Theo Verbeek; Paris: Les impressions nouvelle, 1988).

27. See *The Search after Truth*, transl. Thomas M. Lennon and Paul J. Olscamp, together with a translation of the *Elucidations* (i.e. the Clarifications) plus a Philosophical Commentary by T. M. Lennon (Columbus: Ohio State University Press, 1980).

28. John Christian Laursen, *Journal of the History of Philosophy*, XXXIX, 2001, p. 146.

29. See the excellent study by Walter Rex, *Essays on Pierre Bayle and Religious Controversy* (Den Haag: Martinus Nijhoff, 1965).

30. *Pierre Bayle, Political Writings*, ed. Sally L. Jenkinson (Cambridge: University Press, 2000), Editor's Introduction, p. xxxviii. See also Thomas M. Lennon, *Reading Bayle* (Toronto: University Press, 1999).

31. Foucher is discussed extensively in Richard A. Watson, *The Breakdown of Cartesian Metaphysics* (Atlantic Highlands: Humanities Press, 1987).

32. Bayle, *Dictionary*, article *Zeno of Elea*, Remark F. Popkin, *Selections*, p. 357–358.

33. *Dictionary*, Remark G. Heading: "Objections against the Existence of Extension." Popkin, *Selections*, p. 372.

34. Bayle's references are to Malebranche's *De la Recherche de la vérité*, Clarification (*Eclaircissement*) Six.

35. *Dictionary*, Third Clarification, entitled: "What has been said about Pyrrhonism in this dictionary cannot be harmful to religion." Popkin, *Selections*, pp. 421, 423.

36. See her brilliant study: Elisabeth Labrousse, *Pierre Bayle, Tome II, Heterodoxie et rigorisme* (Den Haag: Martinus Nijhoff, 1964). See especially ch. 2, "La transposition de la méthode cartésienne en Histoire." Labrousse's is the most important study of Bayle. But see also these important works: Ruth Whelan, *The Anatomy of Superstition: a study of the historical theory and practice of Pierre Bayle* (Oxford: The Voltaire Foundation, 1989), and Gianni Paganini, *Analisi della fede e critica della ragione nella filosofia di Pierre Bayle* (Firenze: La Nuova Italia Editrice, 1980).

37. Gilbert Ryle, *The Concept of Mind* (London: Hutchinson, 1949).

38. *After Philosophy: End or Transformation?*, eds. Kenneth Baynes, James Bohman, Thomas McCarthy (Cambridge: MIT Press, 1987), p. 466.

39.   Charles Taylor, *Sources of the Self: the Making of the Modern Identity* (Cambridge: Harvard, 1989), pp. 133, 143, 182, 195.

40.   Charles Taylor, "Quebec Focus," in *McGill News* (Spring 1990).

41.   Noam Chomsky, *Powers and Prospects: reflections on human nature and the social order* (Boston: South End Press, 1966), p. 42.

42.   *The Rediscovery of the Mind* (Cambridge: MIT Press, 1992), p. 100.

43.   *Mental Reality* (Cambridge: MIT Press, 1994), p. 82.

44.   Quoted in John Horgan, *The Undiscovered Mind* (New York: Free Press, 1999), p. 248.

45.   Roger Penrose, *The Large, the Small and the Human Mind* (Cambridge: University Press, 1997), pp. 115–116. See also his *Shadows of the Mind: a search for the missing science of consciousness* (Oxford: University Press, 1994).

46.   From Longair's Foreword to Roger Penrose, *The Large, the Small and the Human Mind*, p. xvi.

47.   David J. Chalmers, *The Conscious Mind: In Search of a Fundamental Theory* (New York: Oxford UP, 1996), p. 330.

48.   Ibid., p. 357.

49.   Jan Koster, personal communication, 27 June 1999. Treating meaning as a category not reducible to matter already appears in Stoic theory, as well as explicitly in the Cartesian, Louis de la Forge's, *Traitte de l'esprit de l'homme* (Paris: Michel & Nicolas Le Gras, 1666). No "likeness" or similarity relation holds between ideas in the mind and the objects they are said to be "about", anymore, he writes, than that between words and things.

50.   Transl. Jenny McPhee and Martha McPhee (New York: Knopf, 1994).

51.   Jonathan Petre, writing for *The Sunday Telegraph*, London. Reprinted in *The Globe and Mail*, Toronto, 27 October 1994.

52.   Aquinas, *Summa Theologica*, Question LXXV, art. iii: "Are the souls of brute animals subsistent?"

53.   John Tillotson, Archbishop of Canterbury, *Works* (9th ed., Dublin: George Grierson, 1726). Sermon xxii.

54.   William Fleetwood, *A Sermon upon Swearing* (London: J. Roberts, 1721).

55.   George Elder Davie has written several profoundly insightful studies on this topic and on the Scottish Enlightenment generally. I am especially indebted to his *The Democratic Intellect: Scotland and her universities in the nineteenth century* (Edinburgh: University Press, 1961), *The Crisis of the Democratic Intellect* (Edinburgh: Polygon, 1986), *A Passion for Ideas: Essays on the Scottish Enlightenment*, Vol II Edinburgh: Polygon, 1994) and *The Scotch Metaphysics: a Century of Enlightenment in Scotland* (London: Routledge, 2001).

56.   How Descartes began to capture the philosophical imagination of Calvinists in the years before the French King abrogated the Edict of Nantes in 1685 is brilliantly discussed by Walter Rex in his *Essays on Pierre Bayle and Religious Controversy* (Den Haag: Martinus Nijhoff, 1965). The guarantees the French Protestants had won in 1596 were valid in perpetuity, but the King ruled that the Edict could be revoked because there were no longer any French

Protestants resident in France! Many tens of thousands of Protestants fled or were expelled. Many were killed.

57. No one has chronicled these arguments with more intellectual rigor and insight than Noam Chomsky. See, for example, "Objectivity and liberal scholarship," and "The responsibility of intellectuals," in his *American Power and the New Mandarins* (New York: Pantheon, 1967), *For Reasons of State* (New York: Vintage, 1973), *Reflections on Language* (New York: Pantheon, 1975). For a direct attack on the behaviorist psychologist B. F. Skinner, see Chomsky's review of Skinner's *Verbal Behavior*, in *Language*, XXXV, 1959, 26–58. See also my *Mind and Language: Essays on Descartes and Chomsky* (Dordrecht: FORIS, 1984).

58. Léon Poliakov, *The Aryan Myth: A history of racist and nationalist ideas in Europe*, transl. Edmund Howard (New York: Basic Books, 1974), pp. 135, 143.

59. James Ussher, Archbishop of Armagh (1581–1656), using biblical sources, calculated that the world had been created in 4004 BC. That date is still employed among some anti-evolutionist fundamentalist groups.

60. A baboon-like animal.

61. David Hume, a footnote to "Essay: of national characters," in *Essays Moral, Political, and Literary*. Hume's Essays began to appear in 1741. This particular Essay first appeared in 1748. This footnote first appeared in the edition of 1753–54.

62. James Beattie, *Elements of Moral Science*, 2 vols. (Edinburgh: William Creech, 1807), cf. Pt II, § 616–656, also his *An Essay on the Nature and Immutability of Truth, in opposition to sophistry and scepticism*, 2nd ed. (Edinburgh: Kincaid and Bell, 1771), Pt II, ch. ii.

63. James Ramsay, *An Essay on the Treatment and Conversion of African Slaves in the British Sugar Colonies* (Dublin: T. Walker, 1784), p. 235.

64. For an introduction to the [European] philosophical background of racism, see Winthrop Jordan, *White over Black: American Attitudes toward the Negro 1550–1812*. (Baltimore: Penguin, 1969).

65. Abbé Henri Grégoire. *De la littérature des negres, ou, Recherches sur leurs facultes intellectualles* (Paris: Maradan, 1808). Francis Hutcheson's, James Ramsay's and Beattie's names are among those the author credits with opposing slavery and fighting for the rights of blacks and mulattoes. Hume's name and hostile opinions are referred to in the text at the beginning of Chapter II.

66. See Richard H. Popkin, *Isaac La Peyrère* (1596–1676) (Leiden: Brill, 1987) for an extended discussion of the father of the Pre-Adamite theory.

67. Gaukroger, *Descartes*, p. 4. In notes to this passage he cites Erica Harth, *Cartesian Women*, (Ithaca: Cornell, 1992), ch. 2, also Peter Schouls, *Descartes and the Enlightenment*, (Kingston, ON: McGill-Queens University Press 1989).

Bibliography

Bracken, Harry M. *Mind and Language: Essays on Descartes and Chomsky.* Dordrecht: FORIS, 1984.

Chomsky, Noam. *Cartesian Linguistics.* New York: Harper and Row, 1966.

Clarke, D.M. *Descartes' Philosophy of Science.* Manchester: University Press, 1982.

Cottingham, J., ed. *The Cambridge Companion to Descartes.* New York: Cambridge University Press, 1992.

Descartes, R. *Oeuvres de Descartes*, eds. Charles Adam and Paul Tannery, 13 vols. Reprinted, Vrin, 1957–. Abbreviated "AT"

——*Oeuvres philosophiques*, ed. Ferdinand Alquié, 3 vols. Paris: Garnier Frères, 1963–73.

——*The Philosophical Works of Descartes*, 2 vols. Transl. Elizabeth S. Haldane and G.R.T. Ross. Cambridge: University Press, 1967. Abbreviated "HR"

——*The Philosophical Writings of Descartes*, 3 vols. Transl. J. Cottingham, R. Stoothoff, D. Murdoch, and A. Kenny. Cambridge: University Press, 1984, 1985, 1991. Abbreviated "CSMK"

Doney, W., and Chappell, V.C., eds. *Twenty Years of Descartes Scholarship, 1960–1984: A Bibliography.* New York: Garland, 1984.

Garber, Daniel. *Descartes' Metaphysical Physics.* Chicago: University of Chicago Press, 1992.

141

Gaukroger, S. *Descartes: An Intellectual Biography*. New York: Oxford University Press, 1995.

Gouhier, H. *La Pensée Métaphysique de Descartes*. Paris: Vrin, 1962.

Kenny, Anthony. *Descartes*. New York: Random House, 1968.

Popkin, R.H. *The Columbia History of Western Philosophy*. New York: Columbia University Press, 1998.

——*The History of Scepticism from Erasmus to Spinoza*. Rev. ed. Berkeley/Los Angeles: University of California Press, 1979.

Sebba, G. *Bibliographia Cartesiana: A Critical Guide to the Descartes Literature 1800–1960*. Den Haag: Martinus Nijhoff, 1964.

Shea, William R. *The Magic of Numbers and Motion: the Scientific Career of René Descartes*. Canton, MA: Watson Publishing, 1991.

Watson, R.A. *The Downfall of Cartesianism 1673–1712*. Atlantic Highlands, NJ: Humanities Press International, 1987.

Wilson, Margaret Dauler. *Descartes*. London: Routledge & Kegan Paul, 1978.

Index

INDEX